THE DOMESDAY INHERITANCE

THE DOMESDAY INHERITANCE

Jack Ravensdale

With photographs by Richard Muir

SOUVENIR PRESS

First published 1986 by Souvenir Press Ltd,
43 Great Russell Street, London WC1B 3PA

ISBN 0 285 62749 X

Photoset in Great Britain by
Rowland Phototypesetting Ltd,
Bury St Edmunds, Suffolk and
printed in Great Britain by
BAS Printers Ltd., Over Wallop, Hampshire

For D.J.W.

Contents

Acknowledgements

The author and publisher express their thanks to the following:

Characters in the narrative itself, the great administrators of Corpus Christi College, Cambridge, men zealous in their care of the inheritance descended from the Domesday manor of the Norman sheriff, Picot.

The Master and Fellows of Corpus Christi College for access to the Parker Library and the Landbeach archives; successive Librarians and the Archivist, Mrs C. P. Hall, for years of unstinted help.

The County Archivist and the Librarian of the Cambridgeshire Collection for help far beyond the call of duty over many years.

Dr Richard Muir for so many beautiful photographs, and for the pleasure of working with such a craftsman and scholar.

For permission to reproduce copyright and other material: the Syndics of Cambridge University Library for the extracts from the Domesday Book and the Probate Inventories; the Cambridge Antiquarian Society for the engravings of the Easter Sepulchre and the plan of the church; the Syndics of the Cambridge University Press for their very generous permission to make free use of material from *Liable to Floods*; BBC Publications for the map on p. 25 from *History on Your Doorstep*; the Committee for Aerial Photography for the photographs on pp. 24, 58 and 156; the Rector and Churchwardens of Landbeach for the Parish Documents.

Thanks above all to the scholar whose steadfast interest has made the book possible, Jill Waterhouse.

List of Illustrations

COLOUR PLATES

BLACK AND WHITE PHOTOGRAPHS

LINE ILLUSTRATIONS

1

From Conquistadors to Landlords

A crow flying north from Cambridge takes the line of the old Roman road, the Akeman Street of the antiquarians. Five miles along this track the level of the land drops to form the first fields of the old fens in the little parish of Landbeach, which straddle the boundary between upland and fen, south of the Isle of Ely. From the air can be seen an astonishing sequence of the traces, layer upon layer, of past societies. The community that had settled before the Norman Conquest, and which was described in the Domesday Book, has lived on continuously without a break through all manner of change: growth, decay and renewal, and the physical pattern of the village today is the result of its entire history.

But literate men took a larger part than was common in directing the ways of life in Landbeach. Literate men generate documents, value and preserve them, whereas pre-literate or illiterate societies speak to us mostly from their graves. The sticks and stones of history have come into their own more in recent years. Church and chapel, house and barn, ditches and banks, roads and paths all tell their own stories, and every village today contains the materials for its own biography in its physical make-up. But much of the life of the past cannot be recalled unless we have documents that speak to us directly in words, in human language. In all these sources Landbeach is unusually rich. It is not for nothing that for centuries the lord of the principal manor has been the Master and Fellows of a Cambridge college, that generations of capable and learned men have paid attention to the affairs of the humble men and women who lived here. Not content with an archive in the College that can rarely be rivalled by a village, the former contents of its fine old parish chest are scarcely to be equalled, and all this only comes to tell the history of the village when based on the foundation of the Domesday Book.

It was natural, therefore, that when the eighteenth-century historian of Corpus Christi College, Robert Masters, Rector of Landbeach, turned his attention to writing the village history, even though he never achieved his aim, he started by having his friend and rival supply him with the appropriate extracts from his transcription of Domesday. This comes down to us pasted into the front of Masters' documentary collection, *Collectanea de Landbeach*, of materials for the projected volume. When we look at the richness of this compilation and the elegance of Masters' *Short Account of the Parish of Waterbeach*, we can only wonder at what we have missed.

*   *   *

After the Conquest in 1066, for some years the Normans lived in England uneasily, as an army of occupation. For a while the invaders faced constant threat of assassination; every thicket or clump of reeds might hold a murderously resentful Saxon. The crack of a twig could mean, as it did to other French speakers six centuries later in hostile Canada, the possible menace of a deadly missile. But hopeless resistance loses heart, and eventually fades away.

By 1085 the great rebellions, like that of Hereward, had been defeated. William wanted to count the spoils from the Conquest, and to set up in detail the machinery of the future government, and this, too, he wanted to be as lucrative as he could make it. It was high time that he knew what resources he could count on. Saxon government had invented procedures which must have appealed to him strongly: royal commands going out as letters (writs) to a royal officer (sheriff) in every shire, that would be replied to, even if they demanded extra tax.

Wealth came from land, and all income, directly or indirectly, was drawn from it. William had paid his thugs and half-settled pirate stock with what they wanted, land. He regarded all the land as his, claiming, and possibly believing, that he had inherited it all from Edward the Confessor and conquered it all from Harold. In the course of the campaigns William had made on-the-spot grants to those who needed immediate pay to stay moderately loyal. He made grants of whole estates of Saxon thegns, and his followers found themselves with land-holdings scattered far and wide, unsurveyed and often only identifiable by the names of the Saxons who had held them previously. If this was less than satisfactory for the new Norman lord, it scarcely appealed to William who wanted his tax-collectors to know who to assess for each holding of land. Furthermore, he wanted to build up as powerful a modern army as he could, and needed land to grant in return for service by fully armed

1 A curious figure in the East window of Landbeach parish church. Is he an imaginative reconstruction of King Harold?

and equipped mounted knights. Those who held land directly from the King, his tenants-in-chief, or barons, in their turn granted land to be held in return for producing its fruits in cash, kind or labour. Thus, when the Domesday Book was finally assembled, the country was described county by county in lists of what was held by each of the barons, the 'Holders of Lands'. So we arrive at a picture of a society organised to provide and feed the largest possible army, a society thoroughly militarised.

In the days of uncertainty in almost any locality, overmighty barons, especially if they were royal officials, might oppressively seize and hold land of lesser men and hope to get away with it. This was especially true of Picot, the Norman sheriff of Cambridgeshire. The Church, without military power, was particularly vulnerable. The Anglo-Saxon Chronicler described him with nice precision: 'A roving wolf, a crafty fox, a greedy hog, a shameless dog, one who feared not God nor St Etheldreda (Patron Saint of Ely Diocese, foundress and first Abbess of the Abbey of Ely)— indeed he declared he had never heard of her.'

The uncertainty and the readiness of local magnates to resort to force meant that precise knowledge of property rights was needed if right was to be done, law and order kept and the King's resources husbanded. At each of the three great Christian festivals of the year William wore his crown at an especially full meeting of his Council at which the great

15

policy decisions were taken. At Christmas 1085, he was, as usual, at Gloucester, and there 'he had deep speech with his Witan' (the Saxon name for the Council—Wise Men), according to the Chronicler. It was at this meeting that the great survey was planned.

Commissioners were to be sent out into every shire to discover and bring back the amounts and value of land and livestock. Their results were to be checked by a second party of commissioners who would go to places which they did not know, and where they were themselves unknown.

Their method of collecting the information required was by one of the tools of mediaeval administration, the inquest or inquisition, a sworn jury answering questions on oath. The knowledge that William wanted was scattered throughout the country. In every place the old men had learned the rights and wrongs of local land-holding as they grew up, and old men on oath, getting closer to the next world, would answer truly. Where title had been in question in living memory they would have known.

The original intention to include an account of stock seems to have been dropped in most places before the final compilation. The main Domesday volume, which looks to have been the work of one copyist, appears to have dropped it, but the second volume, the work of a number of scribes, and some of the subsidiary documents, often still record it. Questions about livestock seem to have worried the Anglo-Saxon Chronicler. In his words we hear something of the fear of an illiterate peasantry having to answer highly personal questions and seeing their answers put down in writing: 'So very narrowly did he have the survey made that there was not one hide of land, not a yard, not—and shame it is to say what he thought no shame to do—not even a single ox or cow or one pig but was recorded in writing.' The jurors, especially the Saxon ones, must have been in terror. The least they could have expected was a swingeing tax.

Domesday normally records by name those who hold land directly from the King. Sometimes Saxon 'antecessors' are also so dignified in order to identify the land in question—for example, Blacuin the Saxon sheriff is named where his Norman successor, Picot, has enlarged the sheriff's estate by seizing land from poor men and the Church. The future manor of Chamberlains in Landbeach had been more than doubled in its land after passing to Picot.

The lesser social classes were given as numbers only, and we usually assume that these numbers probably represent heads of households, mostly with at least some land to cultivate for themselves.

As well as the two volumes of the official Domesday Book there are a number of subordinate 'satellite' surveys. Much of South-west England is covered by the Exon Domesday. The Monks' Domesday deals with the estates of Christchurch Priory at Canterbury. The Feudal Book of Bury St Edmunds is similar. Much of Cambridgeshire has two additional sources of Domesday material: the Ely Inquest, concerned with the estates of the Abbey of Ely, and the Inquisition for Cambridge County.

This last-mentioned survey works through the material, moving from one hundred (the local government division within the shire or county) to the next. It breaks off in its account of Madingley, just before Landbeach would have been dealt with. A little extra material on Landbeach would have been useful, since scholars have created a problem of distinguishing between Landbeach and Waterbeach. In the Domesday Book the former is called Utbech, and the latter Bech. The great eighteenth century antiquarian, William Cole, and his Landbeach rival, Robert Masters, who once employed him as curate in Waterbeach, kept in touch. Cole supplied Masters with a transcript of what he thought was the Domesday entry for Landbeach. Masters duly copied this out in his *Collectanea* (really a scholar's scrapbook), and there it remains, in Masters' hand, a reasonably accurate text of the Landbeach entries. When Cole transcribed the Waterbeach entries he sent these also to Masters, 'just in case'. Masters accepted them with gratitude, and fixed Cole's letter, containing the less successful transcripts, with sealing-wax over the correct version in his own hand. The difficulty in distinguishing between the two villages as the forms of the name changed in time, has now entrapped the editor of the Cambridgeshire volume of a recent edition, where the identifications are again reversed. The later descent of the manors makes it quite clear that in Domesday Bech is Waterbeach and Landbeach is Utbech.

The reverse identification produces some absurdities, like a rent of 1,450 eels per year from Landbeach where only the tip of the parish is fen, while Waterbeach, a handful of islands in an enormous fen, pays none.

In spite of all the difficulties and imperfections of the Domesday Book, it is a most remarkable document; for all its omissions and puzzles, no other country could rival it for centuries. It very rapidly became a source of title to most land in England. It soon acquired a popular reputation, and created something like a folk-law of its magic powers to prove the unprovable. By reckoning the whole country in categories derived from continental lawyers, and far too simple for much of English rural life to be fitted into, and then using this to judge land disputes, an almost invisible process began of fitting the English into a Procrustean bed.

*   *   *

E Libro de Domesday

In Beche fuit quidam Sochm. qui habuit s. virg de
Soc. Ste Ethed. de Eli, & modo habet Walterus de comite
Alano, valet 5.ˢ

In Utbece Mucellus de Picot Vicecomite s. virg de Soca s.ᵃ Etheld. de Eli: potuerit vendere sine soca, valet
3ˢ. et in eadem Villa tenuerunt Ailbertus de st Ethel.
de Eli s. Hid. non potuit vendere nec ab Ecclesia separare; et modo habet pred: Mucellus de Picot vicecomite,
valet 10.ˢ

In eadem Villa tenent 2 Carpentarii 3 hid. et dim.
qui tenet Osuni de Sᵗ Etheld. de Eli nec possunt vendere nec ab Eccles.ᵃ separare ut totus hund. testatur,
T. R. E. et in mort ejus valet 3 lib. . . . . .

Bp. Montacute granted a licence to Hen. Chamberlayne
to have Mass said in his own House 1339.

Land-Beach All Saints.

IS a Rectory in the Hundred of *North-Stowe* and Deanry of *Chesterton*, valued
in the King's Books at 10*l.* 1*s.* 3*d.* It pays a Pension to the King of 40*s*; for
Tenths 1*l.* 1*d.* ¾ and for Procurations 2*s.* 6*d.* In Domesday Book it is called *Beche*
— *Utbece* — *Uthbeche* and sometimes *Udbecce*, ~~and~~
Waterbeche the adjoining Parish. In the time of *Nigellus* Bp. of *Ely* about 1140,
William ——— and *Bernard* ——— were Priests here. The Church was appropri-
ated to *Bernewell* Priory by *William Longchamp*, and confirmed by his Successor
Eustathius about 1200; when *Bartholomew* ——— Clerk was Rector. In 1290
the Church was taxed at 10*l*, the Portion of the Prior of *Bernewell* at 1*l*, and his
Goods

2 : 0 : 0 ₶
1 : 0 : 1 ¾
0 : 3 : 4
1 : 12 : 0
0 : 2 : 10

viz. Waterbeche
of Watbeche

It is taxed at 110₶ — * of Coppied Hall Close here
with a Legin of Parson's Close,

the Cow yard & part of the Garden or Orchard is leased by Mr. Spencer as far as for
the Sale thereof to the Dove cote & Walls of s.ᵈ House at 20.ˢ p̄ an —
A Leg on ye side of ye Day some gt. Hou se, & at 12.ˢ for Coming into Orchard
B of upper end of Close — & Clause in s.ᵈ Lease —

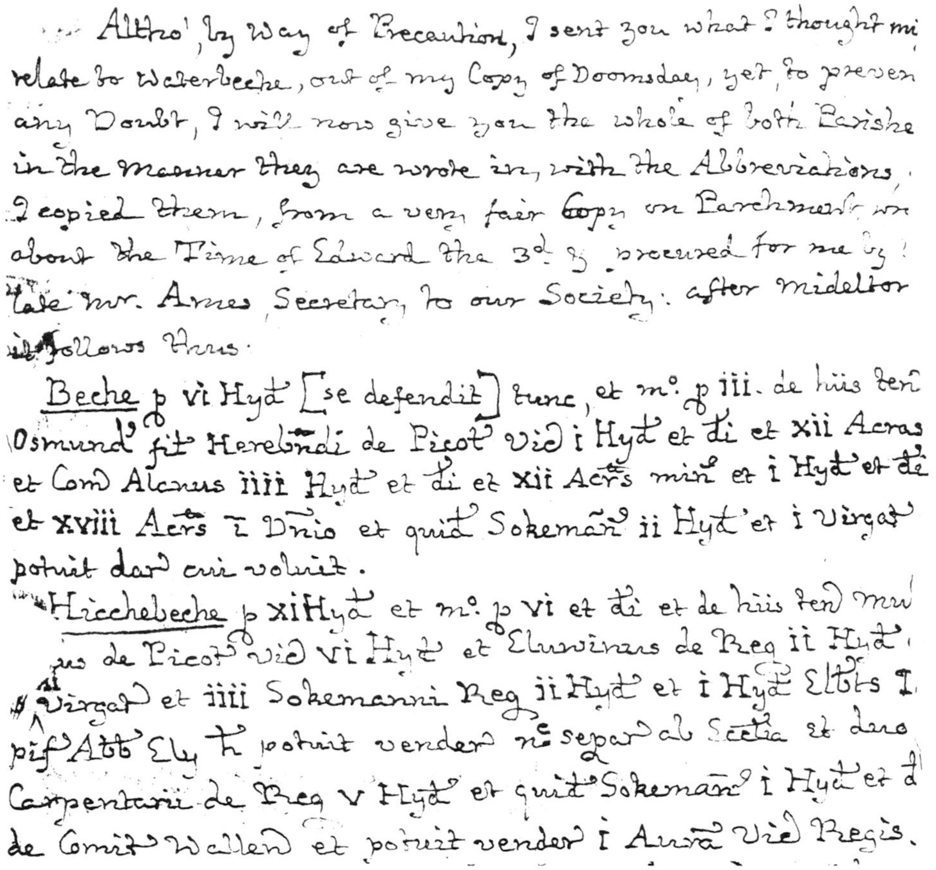

... Altho', by Way of Precaution, I sent you what I thought mi relate to Waterbeche, out of my Copy of Doomsday, yet, to preven any Doubt, I will now give you the whole of both Parishe in the manner they are wrote in, with the Abbreviations. I copied them, from a very fair Copy on Parchment wr about the Time of Edward the 3d & procured for me by late Mr. Ames, Secretary, to our Society: after Midelton it follows thus.

Beche p vi Hyd [se defendit] tunc, et mo. p iiii. de hiis ten Osmund fit Herebrndi de Picot vid i Hyd et di et xii Acras et Com Alanus iiii Hyd et di et xii Acrs min et i Hyd et de et xviii Acrs I Dnio et quid Sokeman ii Hyd et i Virgat potuit dar cui voluit.

Hicchebeche p xi Hyd et mo. p vi et di et de hiis ten mu us de Picot vid vi Hyd et Eluuinars de Reg ii Hyd & Virgat et iiii Sokemanni Reg ii Hyd et i Hyd Eltbts I pif Abb Ely h potuit vender ñ separ ab Sctia et dero Carpentarii de Reg v Hyd et quid Sokeman i Hyd et d de Comit Wallen et potuit vender i Aura vid Regis.

It is not very clear to what extent the manor had become the dominant institution of the English countryside before the Conquest. When Seebohm was investigating the *English Village Community* in the midnineteenth century, his quick comment on mediaeval England was 'manors everywhere'. He was followed by Maitland in *Domesday Book and Beyond*: 'Manors, manors, everywhere'. The Domesday clerks, trying to classify, had created.

The two manors in Landbeach appear to be made up chiefly of a baffling variety of sub-tenants, with complex and subtle variations of status and degrees of freedom, and different degrees of obligation to their lords. The manor that later passed to the Chamberlain family, and later still to Corpus Christi College, Cambridge, where it still remains, had six villeins, four bordars and nine cottars. The villeins held most land and paid for it largely through a heavy rent in labour. The other two classes had less land (the cottar may simply have had a cottage). It has been argued that at this time the term villein only meant villager, and that the connotation of unfreedom only came later. This is a little hard to accept. In what sense can a villein be free if he is not allowed to leave the manor without permission of his lord?

Fig. 1 (*opposite page*) From Robert Masters' *Collectanea de Landbeach*, William Cole's transcription of the Domesday entry for the Landbeach area, copied in Masters' hand.

Fig. 2 William Cole's second attempt, in his own manuscript hand.

19

a. XXXVIII The Land of two Carpenters of the King. In Norestou Hundred In Utbech two Carpenters hold from the King 5 hides. There is land for 2 ploughs and a half. In demesne there are 4 hides and 1 virgate and there are 2 ploughs there. There 3 villeins with 10 cottars have half a plough. It is worth 110 shillings; when received £4 10 shillings; in the Time of King Edward £7 10 shillings. A man of Earl Waltheof held 1½ hides of this land, and provided one carrying service, and could sell the land; and Oswius, the man of the Abbot of Ely, held 3½ hides and could neither sell nor separate them from the Church, as the men of the Hundred testify.

b. In Utbech Muceullus holds from Picot 6 hides, and there is land for 3 ploughs; 1 is on the demesne; and 6 villeins, with 4 bordars and 9 cottars have 2 ploughs. Meadow for 3 ploughs and pasture for the cattle of the vill. It is worth £4 and 6 shillings; when received £3; in the Time of King Edward £4 and 10 shillings. Of this land Blacuin held 2 hides and 3 virgates from the King, and 4 men of King Edward had 2 hides and provided 3 carrying services and a watchman for the sheriff; and Albert, the man of the Abbot of Ely, had 1 hide which he could neither sell nor separate from the Church; and another man of the Abbot had 1 virgate and could sell it but the soke remained to the Abbot.

Some technical terms:
Picot was the Norman sheriff of Cambridgeshire. Blacuin was his Saxon predecessor.
Hide = 120 acres as assessed for tax.
Virgate = ¼ hide, 30 acres.
Villein = unfree tenant who held land in exchange for labour services.
Bordars and Cottars = lesser peasant tenants.
Soke = right of jurisdiction, or land over which such right runs.

One interesting suggestion as to the exact significance of the term 'bordar' is that it represents peasants who were allowed to settle on the edge of the field and forest, who were largely responsible for the great woodland clearances of this period. It would then fit with the continental French term. It seems to drop out of usage by the thirteenth century, when we may presume that forest clearance was over.

With the information in Domesday about the pre-Conquest population, we rarely seem to have anything that can be thought of as a complete list of householders in the way that the later peasant lists appear complete, but instead we seem to get a subtle gradation of free and unfree status: men who can sell their land; men who can go with their land to a new lord; men who can sell their land but still come under the jurisdiction of the lord; men who can sell their land but the jurisdiction over the land remains to the same lord.

On the future Chamberlains manor six men with various degrees of late Saxon modified freedom occupied the place taken over before 1085 by nineteen villeins and lesser holders. As one looks at village after village across the great change of the Conquest, it becomes less and less possible to escape from the conclusion that the Normans depressed the status of most of the English peasantry and that the next two centuries made matters worse until the terms villein and serf became synonymous. In Domesday Landbeach had no serfs, although there had been some in neighbouring Cottenham. The term then meant quite simply 'slave'.

The second Domesday manor in Landbeach, which comes down to us as the manor of Brays, is very distinctive in that it is held directly from the King by two of the King's Carpenters. We know no more about them, nor why they should be so privileged, but it was on the fen edge, just to the north of Landbeach parish, at Cotingelade, Cottenham Lode, that William assembled his invasion craft for the assault on the Isle of Ely held by Hereward. Carpenters from Landbeach could, at that time, have rendered invaluable service to him. Timber assault towers were prepared against the defenders. In one a witch, employed to curse the Saxons, perished when the Saxons tossed a lighted torch into the reeds. A pontoon bridge, which sank under the panicking Normans, might well have been of their construction.

There would seem to have been a tradition of wood-working in Landbeach. In the fifteenth century Nicholas Toftys of Landbeach was employed by the lord of the principal manor, Corpus Christi College, to re-roof their hall, and probably the same man was responsible for the fine roof from the same period in the village church. Landholding like this, for non-military service, was termed petty serjeanty.

The two carpenters in the Domesday Book stand as 'lords' over a 'manor' which has a population of but simple men of small possession. The carpenters kept most of their arable for themselves, and probably had little help in labour rents from their tenants. The bulk of the population are cottars, ten of them. Virtually landless, they probably lived on the rich and varied produce of the fens, fishing, fowling, basket-making. If this little estate, as we can see it in 1086, could only be a manor to someone whose head was already stuffed full of manors, in 1066 it was even less well formed. Then it was unevenly divided. Three tenths were held in petty serjeanty, in this case for a carrying service by a man of Earl Waltheof of Huntingdon and Northumberland. The Earl joined in the revolt against William and was executed in 1076. The other seven tenths were held by Oswius, whose lord was the Abbot of Ely, and although Oswius was probably free personally, his land was not. The men who worked it had to hold it directly or indirectly from the Abbot. It would have taken the special knowledge of the lawyers of the time to recognise that the land of the King's Carpenters constituted a manor.

The other estate, which was held by the sheriff, the Saxon Blacuin before the Conquest and the Norman Picot after, was set a little more clearly in manorial mould. Picot let it out entire to Muceullus, who retained about one third of the arable for his own cultivation. This he should have been able to cultivate by the labour rents of the villeins, his unfree dependants, who would have worked most of the rest themselves. Again there is a disproportionately large group of smallholders or land-less, four bordars and nine cottars. This is characteristic of fen-edge villages. Muceullus is in our terms a modest tenant farmer, and his lordship of the manor is not to be interpreted in any aristocratic sense.

2

On the Far Side of Domesday

Before Domesday could leave an inheritance it received one. Man had begun to shape the area known now as Landbeach long before. The place had shown that it could change to fit the society of those who came to sojourn or to settle and put down roots. Nearby, early prehistoric farmers had cleared the scrub and tilled the rich peaty soil on the edge of the swamp-lands, losing and leaving behind their axes and hoes of polished stone. Permanent settlement and exploitation of the land came much later, and then, with one major break, continued until today.

Aerial photography has revealed Iron Age settlement, probably in part pre-Roman but reaching right through until after the Legions had been withdrawn. In the south-east quadrant of the village a profusion of potsherds, numerous coins and a tangle of silted ditches suggest a small village rather than a single farmstead. Standing a little back from the edge of the fen, and above the critical level of the great flood of the third century, it lasted well into the fifth. Ditches of what seems to be the same period extend through the present village northwards towards the fen. A garden near the cross-roads produced not merely a Roman *dupondius* (a coin rather like a thick halfpenny), but also a prehistoric axe. Levelling the field in the centre of the village to make a recreation ground discovered an Iron Age ditch running under a mediaeval hollow-way. Cultivation of the now drained fen at the north end of the village reveals the line of the Roman Road in the dark parallel lines of silted ditches, joined by feeder roads running in from both sides.

Other dark lines of small enclosures, and what may have been fish-traps in the shallow waters of the swamps from the days before fen drainage, suggest that we have much more to learn from the ground beneath our feet.

The first settlement of the area was planted firmly on the lighter gravelly soil that in the Middle Ages was to become Banworth Meadow, and Banworth Field, and which at this time was exploited by mixed farming. Somewhat later, the Roman colonisation of the fen-edge may have been instigated by the Imperial Government itself to produce wool, tallow, hides and leather, as well as corn, to clothe and feed the garrison of the north, first at Lincoln and later at York. Serving this purpose the Car Dyke was dug, providing a waterway from the productive fens to the insatiable military machine in the north, poised ready to cut off and destroy any irruption of barbarians coming down across Hadrian's Wall.

The waterway linked the Cam and Ouse, cutting through the low gravelly watershed near another splendid Roman farm site in Cottenham fens at Bullocks Haste. The central, highest section was fed by the never-failing waters since diverted into the Beach Ditch. The design

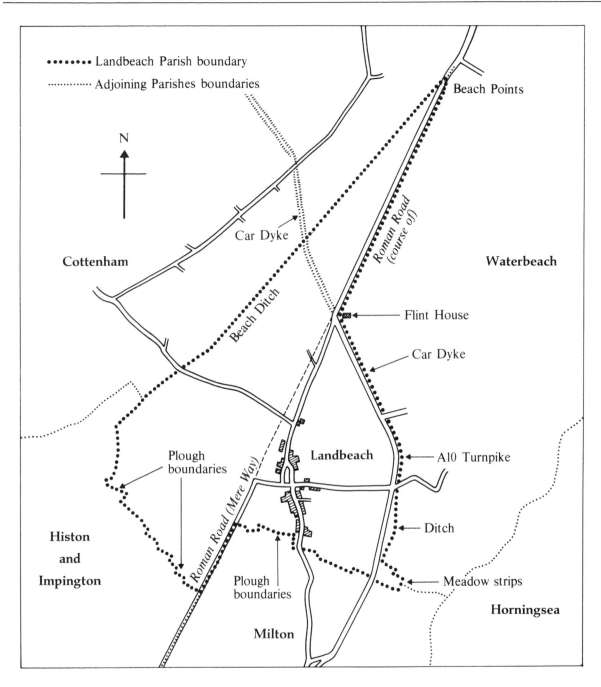

Fig. 3 The Parish of Landbeach. Most of the parish boundaries—the Roman road and canal and a short stretch of watercourse—would have been found already there by the first Saxons to arrive. The rest—plough boundaries, meadow strips and the Beach Ditch—were all the result of dividing 'no-man's land' with neighbouring villages during the Middle Ages. *Reproduced by kind permission of BBC Publications from* History on Your Doorstep.

shows that the canal, normally fifteen feet wide, between berms each a further fifteen feet wide, must have been a fairly sophisticated piece of hydraulic engineering, with some sort of locks to control the water's flow and level. This contrasts with the mediaeval ditches, which merely followed the course of natural drainage, accepting limited cross-country navigation or adopting what the Romans had left.

The other route to the north, probably built by the advancing Ninth Hispana legion in the Emperor Claudius's campaign of conquest in the early 40s of the first century, was the road which later antiquarians called Akeman Street. This was probably used mostly for the mounted police, the Roman cavalry, based in the little walled town on Castle Hill in Cambridge, that protected the tax-collectors, and the postal waggons which took the taxes away to Rome.

About the year 230 AD the Car Dyke seems to have collapsed, only to be partially restored about forty years later. Even then settlement seems to have been less dense. For a time something survived, but at some time in the fifth century the Roman farms seem all to have been abandoned.

In the collapse no one looked after the Car Dyke. The waters of the Cam ran down the course of the canal, adding a dangerous weight in time of flood. The banks of the Car Dyke burst, and the waters made their way around the eastern side of the Isle of Ely. The Old West River was born and the Isle of Ely became an island. Much of the road was also engulfed at the same time, but enough was left to help make the later mould in which the village grew.

After the hiatus at the end of the Roman Empire we can perceive very little before the Domesday Book. What evidence there is is archaeological. Where the Iron Age and Roman farmers had cleared the soil, and they had chosen the lighter areas, these would quite quickly, once abandoned, have reverted to scrub. The heavier soils that relied exclusively on the rivers to take away flood-waters, would probably have become worse than ever when the watercourses began to take their own ways.

The little evidence local place-names can give has to be used for lack of something better. There were, for instance, a number of Saxon names for the canal: Car Dyke itself, which was not used for the Cambridgeshire section until modern antiquarians began to discuss it, meant a waterway overgrown with reeds and shrubby thickets. This makes it clear that the Saxon settlers found a canal system that had been neglected and allowed to revert to wild fen. Other names were *Eldelode*, the old ditch; *Tillage*, *Tilling*, or *Twilade*, which suggests a portage around a collapsed lock involving a second loading. The village name itself, *Beach*, probably refers to a stream, *Beck*, which makes more sense than a shore, even in wetter times. There is a Beck Brook not too far away, showing that the word was current in this area, and this was the meaning and source of the name as given by the jurors of 1459, who drew up the new rental made that year. They indicated a watercourse flowing by the Green 'whence the whole town of Beach gets its name'.

After the Roman occupation was over and the area was again settled by people from the Continent, there seems to have been a pattern of mother and daughter villages; for example, Barton, the barley or corn village, contrasted with the Cote village, Coton, the sheep settlement. In the same way, judging by later inter-common rights, Rampton probably began as a dependency of Willingham, and Westwick of Cottenham, even though in the early fourteenth century Oakington was able to claim Westwick. The name means western dairy-farm in a period when our local dairies were predominantly sheep.

The area that was to become Landbeach was on the whole situated a little higher than Waterbeach, and much of it was composed of well-drained gravels. This made it an ideal place for the flocks of Waterbeach to graze, especially when rising water threatened them nearer home. The names, Dunstall (town-stall) and Moorman, seem to hint at the early process of reclamation out on the edge of the old forest. Here the beasts would have begun to tame the wild landscape before the axe had got rid of the trees; before the plough had begun to convert them to open field.

When the black waters of the fen rose, Waterbeach would have become a small and very crowded island. The shepherds watched and waited as the winter floods ebbed away until it was suitable for a return home. Sooner or later, the white waters of a sudden or extraordinary flood rushing down from the upland catchment area would fail to clear for one or two seasons, and the higher and drier outline of the old Romano-British settlement, standing proud of the floods, would have invited settlement which lasted, and looks like lasting, for a long time yet.

The field name *Banworth* probably goes back to the days when the shepherds were only making seasonal visits from the ground near the river, but could make the first tentative efforts at supplementing their diet with quick-growing beans in the easily worked light soil. In any spring when flooding threatened the main harvest down by the river, a late-sown crop of beans on the land that cleared of water first could produce a crop in the lean months before harvest, and provide something to eke out that harvest if it were meagre. It could supplement the meat and cheese which were the normal contribution to the diet from the shepherd's flocks.

The change from being a seasonal outstation of the settlement of Waterbeach, to a village in its own right, was probably associated with the heavy task of forest clearance on the clay, that accompanied the start of arable farming with a full team of oxen, and a plough that undercut the sod, turning it right over.

Our clues to the establishment and development of Landbeach's system of open fields come mainly from names in the land charters. There are some 120 of these surviving for Landbeach. Many describe in detail land being transferred from one person to another. The earliest we have date from the thirteenth century. None of these tells us directly what kind of field system is in operation; many have hints. The earliest are often at pains to deal with three equal portions of land, suggesting that something like a common midland system was in operation. Much later the plough-land of the village was described as 'lying in three parts, two corned, one close'. Domesday's figures of ploughlands, if they mean anything, suggest that the fields had already developed most of their estimated potential.

The first field-name given in a charter is from the thirteenth century, *Acrefeld*, on the west of the High Street, south of the cross. The name indicates land ploughed in ridge and furrow, and does not distinguish it from any other mediaeval ploughing. It appears to be the area first ploughed as the daughter settlement developed its own arable. But quite early its name changes to a better designation, *Stratefeld*, the field with the Roman road. When another field develops in the north, across the part of the Roman road there, yet another change of name takes place to *Millfeld*, the windmill having been there since before 1316.

The early fourteenth century saw disastrous rains and floods. The northern field which had been established against the fen began to suffer flooding and encroachment from the fen waters. For a time land in Banworth meadow was ploughed and cropped to bring back a balance. But Banworth itself began to flood in its lowest parts. In desperation the plough came into operation in Hardmede, the very dry meadowland that had been shared between Landbeach, Waterbeach and Milton. It still remained *Meadowfield* even after it had long gone back to grass. The western moor was added to the adjacent fields, *More under Dunstall*, and *Scachbow in Morefield*.

When the pressures of fenland floods eased later in the century, Banworth still cropped with Scachbow, and continued to do so after other temporary arable had gone back to grass; indeed it did so until the enclosure of 1813.

Landbeach's field system grew and developed for the most part inside clear features which were to become boundaries of the parish. Two long sections are from the Roman road, and one from the Roman canal, the Car Dyke. An old watercourse which probably ran into the canal marks the southern part of the eastern boundary, and the extreme south-eastern

28

corner is made up from straight strips of land which give away the site of the old Hardmede. Two sections of the southern boundary are from where the ploughs met with those of Milton; the other long boundary on the western side looks almost straight enough to be Roman, but is in fact a boundary ditch dividing the common fen between Cottenham and Landbeach, dug in 1235. It is still known as Beach Ditch, and the lane alongside as Hay Lane, from the hedge authorised at the same time. (*Haia*, Latin 'hedge'.)

4 The Beach Ditch, dug in 1235 as a boundary dividing the common fen between Cottenham and Landbeach. Hay Lane runs alongside.

This was late for the establishment of boundaries, but further north in the deep fens, where boundaries were so difficult to mark, the divisions between some of the parishes were not always complete until relatively recent times. The ditch of 1235 finally fixed Landbeach's allocation of fen ground. The peculiar long thin wedge of land, similar to that of Rampton, again suggests that latecomer Landbeach was given the leftovers when Waterbeach and Cottenham, long established, were satisfied.

The arable land was ploughed in 'ridge and furrow'. The ridge could be called an 'acre', or a 'land', or a host of other names, but the proper technical term in most of our documents is 'selion', a French term probably imported by Norman French lawyers. This was the unit of ploughing. A man's holding in the field would be made up of scattered strips each of one or more selions. Bundles of these strips with the selions usually all parallel were called 'furlongs' (each one furrow long, otherwise of almost infinite variation). The furlongs were grouped into 'fields' with no hedges or fences to divide them up. In Landbeach we saw how in face of floods Landbeach men improvised something more suited to their conditions than their original simple three-fold system where one field at a time was the unit of rotation. Rather the rotation grouped the disjointed fields as 'Seasons' (called according to their place in the cycle, winter, spring (Lent) and fallow). The complexities were further increased by rights of common grazing over stubbles and fallows, and over mown meadows, as well as other commons. All the cultivators had to follow the common practice and keep to the proper seasons, or grazing beasts would eat their crops. And so there had to be some form of strong local government to make the whole plan work.

3

Running the Village: the Manors

The greater part of the control, administration, planning, maintenance of law and order, public works like roads and drains, was in the hands of the manor court. What happened when there was more than one manor? Historians have sometimes suggested that there was a village court, antedating the manor, going back into Anglo-Saxon times as the Folkmoot. There is very little trace of this, just enough to encourage us in the belief in some occasional sort of popular court, held by an illiterate populace, without benefit of written record. A few direct references to such Courts of the Bi-lawe, or similar, have been found in one or two places elsewhere. Occasionally we get changes in regulations and new orders attributed to all the lords and their tenants, free and unfree, and the whole township. The best evidence in this locality of anything like such a court was on Maundy Thursday 1344. On that day all the lords, their stewards, their tenants free and unfree of Cottenham were summoned to the parish church. There should have been Landbeach men with interests in Cottenham among them. Charters have survived from this meeting. One dealt in minute detail with the laying out of the grass in just shares for the hay harvest; another with the disposal and distribution of shares in the pennies charged by villagers who took in 'foreign' beasts (animals from anywhere over the parish boundary); and the third was a statement of the rights and duties involved in digging peat for fuel in the moor.

Long before this, questions of such magnitude in local life tended to be settled by the King's itinerant justices. But the meeting in the church could possibly be a village court which met *ad hoc* as necessary. If so, it still appears to be using the manorial lords' staff to copy the charters.

From a later period there comes a good deal more evidence of how two manors in one village managed. The early Tudor court rolls of the Landbeach manors reveal instances of ordinances, clearly for the whole village, being passed at the Chamberlains court, but bearing provisos like: these laws to have effect if the other lord's court agree them, and not otherwise.

There were two kinds of manor court, the customary court or the court baron, which dealt only with the unfree tenants, and the court leet and view of frankpledge which dealt with matters of public jurisdiction over freemen as well as bondmen. The view of frankpledge was supposed to be an annual review of the policing system by which every man was to be enrolled in a tithing, a group who were to be responsible for the good behaviour of each other. A lord, in theory, could not hold a leet and view unless he had been granted a specific right by the King. In 1278–9 Agnes de Bray claimed such a right, although the jurors did not know on what authority. Chamberlains also went on exercising such jurisdiction.

The area occupied by Landbeach and its neighbours formed a tangle of inter-locking rights. Not only did most of the villages have more than one manor, but tenants and lords held land from each other so that at the top social level in the village, as well as lower in the hierarchy, the chain of legal obligation became confused and, where barons from outside were involved, often unenforceable.

The Domesday commissioners had no powers or duty to create any hierarchy of manors; it was enough if they reported the chain of lordship over each piece of land which related it to the King, from mesne tenants through tenants-in-chief. (A tenant-in-chief was a baron who held his land directly from the King. His own tenants were called mesne tenants.)

How the rights of a manorial lord were turned into income on the manor of Chamberlains can be seen in astonishing detail for those years in which the account roll survives. A reeve was elected or appointed from the peasantry and, during his office, he was responsible for running the agricultural operations according to local custom, and accounting for all income and expenditure at the annual audit. As well as the major tasks such as ploughing and sowing, reaping and mowing, all the lesser items were accounted for. In 1349 we have particularly rich information surviving because two reeves had to account, the first having been relieved of office after being sick.

Part of the expenditure was incurred in running and maintaining the establishment, and part in payments or gifts made by the lord and lady for extraneous purposes (foreign expenses). There were taxes paid to the sheriff and the King, payment to the clerks and scribes for running the courts, and a few pennies for parchment for the record of the courts and accounts. Almost equal to the payments to the King was an item, 'Paid

to a certain woman for the lady's debt by order of the lord.' Was the woman a dressmaker?

It was a complicated system of accounting. Known as charge and discharge, it spread rapidly in the late thirteenth century when landlords were trying to maximise their incomes in the face of rising prices. It was not quite profit and loss, nor was it designed to indicate investment policy. The reeve was charged with all the assets from the previous year when he took office, every change, for example increase from the harvest, and every payment for house or farm added or deducted as appropriate. It usually ended with the outgoing reeve being charged with arrears which were carried forward to start the next reeve's account. It may not have been a system which modern scientific managers would recommend to take us into the twenty-first century, but it must have saved landlords from gross peculation by amateur local officers.

It would appear that, with the manor court sitting in theory only once a month, and in practice much less, and with only the one annual audit, the possibility of the reeve abusing his power against the interests of both lord and tenant was high.

5 The former home of the parish archives, this fine old chest with its blacksmith-made iron bands, still stands in the church. It has been attributed to the thirteenth or fourteenth century.

Over and against this was the great mediaeval administrative power-house, the villein jury answering most of the vital questions on oath. The most knowledgeable and trustworthy old men, backed up by the almost magical asset, written records that went back beyond the memory of man, constituted a formidable check and balancing force. As far as can now be judged there was rarely much reason to doubt the sworn testimony of a mediaeval peasant jury, in a village where all private life was public, and where the years would have endowed the old men with a minute practical knowledge of local custom which was in fact the local law. Detailed and careful reading of court rolls makes some of the lordly claims seem rather less firmly based than the jury's.

In the Chamberlains manor court of 1332 the jury certainly applied their checking and balancing power to their reeve of two years previous, John Frere. They declared that he had in 1330 taken in the sheaf from the stacks of the lord's corn beyond his due, two bushels of wheat, two bushels of barley, three bushels of peas and one bushel of dredge corn (a mixture of oats and barley). 'And they said further that he had kept a certain foreign woman in the lord's bakehouse, at the lord's expense, although for how long they knew not, and they said further that the same John sent a cartload of the lord's turves to the house of William de Waldersheef in Westwick, where Milsent his concubine was staying.' We should be wary in face of modern parallels.

John Frere was also accused of another piece of sharp practice which seems to have become even more common in the later Middle Ages. He used the lord's fold illegally to compost six acres of other men's land at twopence an acre, when legally it should only have been used on the lord's land.

This example is of checking simple local maladministration. A peasant who felt aggrieved on a point of law could ask (and pay!) for a sworn inquest, and if this failed to settle the point of law, which might be simply that he had for several years been overcharged a farthing a year in rent, he could usually pay for a search in the court rolls to determine the issue finally by uncovering precedent. The combination of sworn jury and written record, from which the Domesday Survey had taken its power, might, perhaps, encourage us to think of the Middle Ages as the Age of Reason. The jury in the manor court declared law as well as fact and in addition presented offenders. The old men of the village would know what was going on. They did, in a pre-literate society, have astonishing memories. Oath-breaking would terrify them. Few ways of coming by the truth can have been more effective.

4

Centuries of Growth

In the Domesday Book we see very few familiar faces. The great tenants-in-chief of the King are named, a few mesne tenants and some of the Saxon antecessors (holders of the land in question before the Conquest) are given names to help firm definition, but virtually all the peasantry are simply counted and reported as a number. In areas like ours, where priests and churches are hardly ever mentioned, some scholars think that priests are included in the numbers of villeins.

The commissioners who were responsible for the area around Ely were instructed (as good civil servants) to report all in triplicate, namely in the time of King Edward, i.e. pre-Conquest; when King William gave the land; and now (1086); but they seem to have taken this seriously only for the valuation of each manor. After all, the government's purpose was surely revealed by the final instruction in the list, 'if it is possible to have more than is had'. Tax officers have a long tradition.

In Landbeach, on Picot's manor, soon to become Chamberlains, there were probably twenty households at the time of the survey. On the land of Two of the King's Carpenters there were probably another fifteen. If we multiply the total households by the probable average family size, thirty-five times four-and-a-half, we arrive at about 157 as the probable order of magnitude of the Landbeach population at Domesday. This is a static estimate, but we can see something of how population increased in the village during the two centuries after Conquest.

When Edward I came to the throne after all the disorder and civil war of Henry III's reign, he commissioned a much more detailed survey than Domesday, although on similar lines. The part for Landbeach of this survives complete in the Hundred Rolls for 1278–9. In this survey, because we have names, we can see problems which the earlier one hid in global numbers, such as the same person holding more than one piece of land, and often holding in more than one manor. By eliminating much of the double-counting in 1278–9 we are probably underestimating the size of the increase. In the later year we seem to have 65 tenant landholders, which suggests a total population for the whole of Landbeach of at least 292; almost double. This is quite consistent with the results of similar calculations for nearby villages. Even an increase of this order is not dramatic if produced over two centuries by a compound rate. But it must have steadily increased the demand for food.

By 1278–9 the names of the manors, as they still survive today, had been received. Brays had passed to that family by 1229, and Chamberlains by 1250. Walter Chamberlain held one knight's fee, and had the right of appointing the rector, or more precisely, presenting the rector for the Bishop to install. The rent of one knight's fee was the obligation to provide one fully armed mounted knight for forty days' service a year. So much detail is given in this later survey that we can observe something of the complex social structure of the English countryside in the high Middle Ages.

Chamberlains' freeholders range from Gilbert Knit, who holds half a knight's fee, to Henry, son of Gilbert, who holds a toft (a small enclosure) containing no more than a single acre. Gilbert Knit appears to have come from one of those families of professional fighting men who settled after the Conquest. He still owed castle guard as part of his rent. They remain a rather superior family in the village for generations, even after the name changes to Lane by descent through the female line. They alone of the tenants receive a share alongside the lords when part of the meadow is ploughed. The land was distributed thirteen selions at a time, six to each lord and one to the Knits. They alone of the tenants seem to share in the overall responsibility for maintaining the canals in the village. There are other hints of ancient survival in the freeholders' rents. Hugh Thurgar holds five acres of arable with pasture rights, for which he pays fourpence and a pair of gloves to John Fitzmore.

Apart from the Prior of Barnwell near Cambridge, who holds thirty acres as an absentee, Chamberlains' other six freemen do not amount to much.

One of Walter's tenants, Thomas Amable, has one small-holding, an acre of toft, and an acre and a half in the arable open field, for which he pays three shillings rent to Denney Abbey, at that time the Hospital for the old veteran Knights Templar, who held the land from Walter. Thomas Amable had another holding of free land from Robert Lucas of a croft (same as toft) of half an acre, and pasture rights that went with it. This Robert held from Gilbert Knit, who held it from Walter, who, of course,

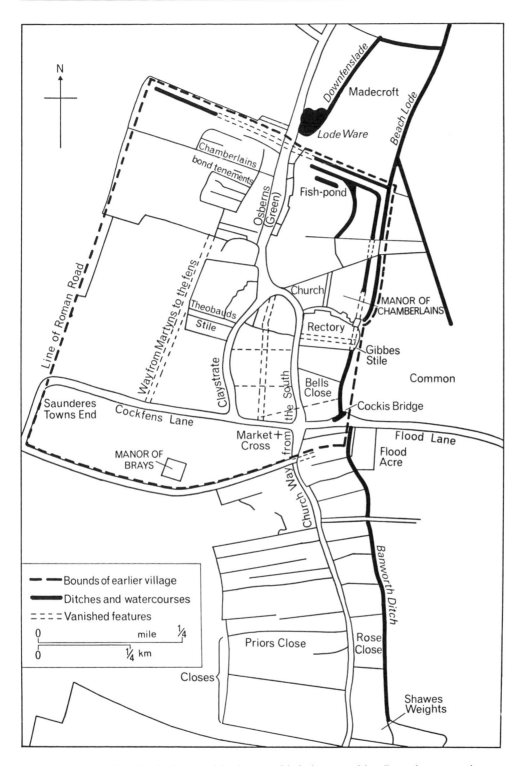

Fig. 4 The Township of Landbeach. The general development of the built-up area of the village is from a squarish settlement in the early Middle Ages, through expansion and contraction to a linear village of the nineteenth century. The north-east corner of the old village shows up clearly on the map as the most vulnerable to floods, and the banks and ditches there appear to be flood defences from the fourteenth century. *Reproduced by kind permission of Cambridge University Press from* Liable to Floods.

37

held from yet another, Gilbert Peche, who held it from the King. Thomas had another holding from Robert Lucas of three acres, for which he paid thirteen pence to Robert, who paid Gilbert Knit twelve pence for it. This method of making a viable small-holding by collecting scraps of land seems to be typical of the fen edge from this time on. In some nearby communities such as Oakington, the process had gone on to the point when such collections of scraps had reached the state where they were claimed as manors.

The danger of obligations to pay tax getting lost in all these complex chains of land-holding led to the government's attempts to restrict the process, and the outline of the manorial arrangements enforced by Domesday are still visible in the early twentieth century as the main constituent source of present patterns of land-holding in the village.

The bulk of the task of increasing output, to meet the steadily growing needs of a rising population, fell on the unfree peasantry as labourers for the lord, and as managers of their villein holdings.

Walter's unfree tenants were listed in two groups, designated villeins and crofters, but within this there were two distinct groups of villeins, eleven holding five acres each, and eight holding only half that amount. The man whose lands and rents were detailed as the type for the five-acre men was John son of Roger who pays 164 works during the year worth 10s.5d., except when they are due on a feast day. In addition he pays:

> 2 chickens worth 2d.
> a capon worth 1½d.
> 5 geese worth 10d.
> He must make 3 quarters of malt for the lord for ½d.
> Carrying services at the will of the lord.

The half villeins (two-and-a-half-acre men) perform 111 weekday works each worth 7s.0d. a year and carrying services at the will of the lord.

All the above services are at the will of the lord (i.e. to take in work or cash as he pleases) unless they fall on festivals or in case of neediness.

The unfree tenants of de Bray are similar:

Agnes has nine five-acre men. They, too, pay, as in the case of Jurdan Atteflood:

> 164 week works worth 10s.5d. and carrying services at the will of the lady.
> 1 chicken worth 1d.
> 2 capons worth 3d.
> 5 geese worth 10d.
> He must make 4 quarters of malt for the lady for ½d.

She also has five half villeins (holding two-and-a-half acres) with Richard Coleville as type. They pay:

> 60 works in the year worth 7s.0d. and carrying services at the will of the lady.
> 1 capon worth 1½d.
> 1 chicken worth 1d.

The lowest economic group of landholders on both the manors, the croftmen, mostly hold nothing more than a cottage in a small croft or toft. Most of them pay cash rent only, often a high rent at that.

Some of the holders and holdings repay close attention that was not possible among the nameless peasantry of Domesday. Luke Shepherd (*Bercator*) is an example. Of Brays manor he held two-and-a-half acres of free land, paying 2s. a year, which was a big enough rent for its time and place. In addition he had a one-and-a-half acre toft from Gilbert Knit paying 4d. and geld (the lord's cash tax instead of knight service). He was probably a professional shepherd for the whole village, with his small-holdings in both manors.

Occupational names in the Hundred Rolls are probably still an indication of profession: Fisher (*Piscator*), Gardener, Smith (*Faber*)—even Knit may be from a regular soldier settled on the land, the knight's fee which he obtained as payment for his military service.

The Landbeach entries show two kinds of surnames derived from place-names: one showing place of origin, de Stanton, Richard Brandon; and the other showing where the family lives in the village. The Attefens disappear only to be replaced by the Fen family who are living at the highest point in the village, as far as possible away from the fens. Floods of the high Middle Ages probably drove them from their old home and sent them to the place safest from the waters. Jurdan Atteflood would have taken his surname from the low place near the cross-roads traditionally called le Floed (spelling optional). On the opposite side of the lane there, lived the Cook or Cox family who had the dock there called Cockis Bridge. Here the lane to Waterbeach was called Flood Lane later on, and the road to the higher part, from Cockis Bridge to Fens Close, acquired the name Cockfen Lane, which never ceases to puzzle because it runs far away from the fens, where the family had dropped the *atte*.

A charter of 1229 refers to a rod of land in Cockfennie, next to the land of Martyn del Fen. This homestead was in a later period to be called Fens Close, or Cockfens and Martyns, or Saunderes Towns End (1459). Cockfens and Martyns closes are listed together by Matthew Parker, Master of Corpus Christi College, Cambridge, when he drew up a list of all the enclosures in the village in the troubled year of 1549. In the naming

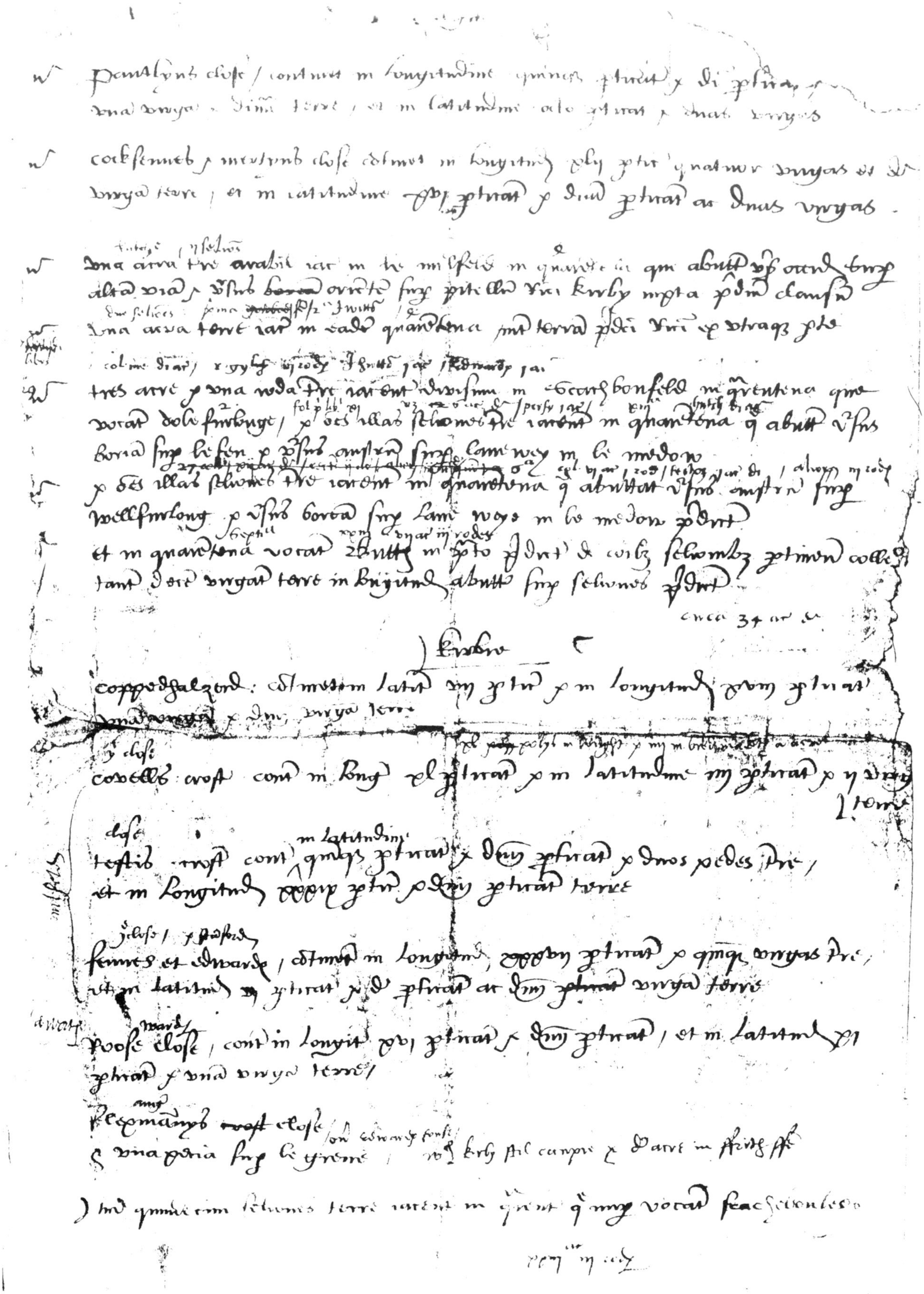

Fig. 5 Matthew Parker's list of all the enclosures in the two manors in 1549. The top half contains those of the College (Chamberlains) and the lower Kirby's (Brays).

of features much of village life is precipitated in village history. In 1377 Roger Sandre (from the family otherwise known as Saunderes) bought his freedom from villeinage from the lord. Villeinage was becoming obsolete, but it survived late in Landbeach, probably because labour services could be taken or 'sold' at the lord's will.

In gaining his freedom he lost his common rights. He was caught when he slipped over the border from Cottenham, where he had moved, and came back to fish in his old haunts. Ten years before Roger was freed, two villeins were sold along with land to another lord. Villeinage had not yet died.

As far as we can trace it, the increase in population in Landbeach in the thirteenth century was probably close to the general pattern. Most mediaeval historians see the thirteenth century as a time when increasing population began to press against the limits of food production. They see something like a Malthusian crisis where population finally became cruelly controlled by famine, pestilence and war, in the first half of the fourteenth century or even earlier, in the late thirteenth century. We could see the general increase in Landbeach between the Domesday Survey and the Hundred Rolls. But it is difficult to pin-point when the upturn ceased and gave way to decline.

Some light is shed by a comparison between what the Hundred Rolls recorded for the manor of Brays in 1278–9 and an even more detailed Survey of the same manor made in 1316.

Survey of 1316 and Hundred Rolls

Source	Freemen	Villeins	Crofters or Cotemen	Tofters or Coterells	
Hundred Rolls	6	9	5	8 (-1)	= 27 or 28
1316	13 (-3 in MD)	12	4 (-1 in MD)	3	= 28 or 32

'in MD' means in the lady's hand

It is very difficult to discern any clear development, but the freeholders seem to have doubled in numbers; as for the full villeins, even though they have increased in numbers by about a third, their average size of holding has also increased, from five to ten acres. Much of this could be the result of breaking in new land, and could include both the land too wet to cultivate and the new ploughing to compensate.

41

There is a strong hint of immigration in the names of the 1316 Survey. Robert le Taylour de Over, John Frost de Waterbeach, Thomas Priest de Cottenham, Richard de Asshewelle, and Robert de Brandon sound like relatively recent arrivals from elsewhere in the region. In the Hundred Rolls there is a Richard Brandon, but none of the others figures there. But there are signs which may mean that Landbeach was far from immune from other trials of the time: against three of the freeholds are notes to say that these are in the lady's hand. These were held by poorer peasants, and 1316 was the great famine year.

The labour services recorded in the Hundred Rolls amounted to 1,476, but in the Survey of 1316 this appears to have risen to 2,363. It does not look as if the Brays manor was suffering from a shortage of workers.

But physical changes and the alteration of the village shape to more of what we can see today, probably come from this period. Expansion to the north was halted against the fen, and was giving ground in face of the renewed attack from the black waters. It was probably about this time that the north-east corner of the village, around the manor of Chamberlains, was protected by banks and ditches which linked measures for flood protection to the commercial canals. These needed a flow to the north to take the laden barges to the main waterways. The new ditches, by increasing the flow and maintaining the water-level later into the spring, would have lengthened the season in which the barges

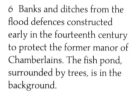

6 Banks and ditches from the flood defences constructed early in the fourteenth century to protect the former manor of Chamberlains. The fish pond, surrounded by trees, is in the background.

could operate. The villeins' carrying services would have taken these narrow boats to and from the local markets and fairs, serving the lord's and lady's needs, and turning the surplus products from the manor into cash. As earlier in Roman times, and later before the Dutchmen took over, drainage and navigation were at their best working together.

The village expanded south along the High Street (*Churchway from the South* in 1459). On the eastern side squarish blocks of land from Banworth were turned into a string of peasant tofts and crofts. This halted short of the parish boundary where part of the meadow was turned to arable to compensate for some of that flooded elsewhere.

In the days of expansion the furlongs alongside the road to the west were taken out of cultivation *en bloc* for building development, and the tell-tale shape made by the mediaeval plough, the faint, reversed 'S' curve, is still to be found there today in some of the property boundaries. The pieces that had not been developed when the Black Death struck and made further building unnecessary, remained as closes until very recent times, and in places the fields still come down to the High Street.

The rhythm of expansion and contraction changed the village by stages to the one we know. The halting of expansion to the north by the fen redirected it to the west as well as the south. The old squarish settlement acquired ribbons of development along Cockfen Lane as well as the High Street. The western part of this almost disappeared at the end of the Middle Ages when the lord of the manor of Brays nearly emptied that part of the village in order to provide himself with paddocks close to home, which he wanted for raising sheep so that he could exploit, or over-exploit, the resources of the fens.

If the two processes of growth and decay left changes such as many other villages have undergone, one feature may have been almost unique to Landbeach: the creation of a mediaeval green in an existing mediaeval village. One of the branches of the Osbern family, who were villeins, had held a croft at the north end of the village. When the last Osbern died, his godson, John Sweyn, worked it for a few years, but about 1429 it was made into a common green by the lord, Corpus Christi College, and at first was called College Green, perhaps to distinguish it from Loo Green, which seems to have been an extension of the village common around the cross-roads.

Part of this went into the grasping hands of Richard Kirby, lord of the manor of Brays early in the sixteenth century. Some encroachment in this area seems to have taken place by building two cottages nearby. These were not, as not being of immemorial foundation, entitled to common rights. Part still survived into the Field Book of 1549 as 'The Little Piece Called Tree at the Cross'.

7 The village Green, created early in the fifteenth century, was allotted as gardens to adjoining houses at the time of the Parliamentary Enclosure.

The sites of both mediaeval manors are marked by substantial moats, that of Brays square and waterfilled: that of Chamberlains dry and complex, behind the churchyard. The tradition identifying these sites is well backed up by documentation and field archaeology. Until the grass field in the middle of the village was levelled to make a playing ground a few years ago, a hollow-way ran down its centre, bisecting it. This can still be seen on the aerial photograph. There were three peasant homesteads on either side. In Brays Court Roll for 1414 the holders are named and the claim asserted that the hollow-way was a path to church for the lord, lady, family, his ministers, servants, and all the tenants. There is a tradition that it was called Paternoster Way.

The dates of building and abandoning the mediaeval manor houses can now be discovered only by archaeological methods, although references to the house of Chamberlains seem to fade out before the College acquired it in 1359.

The Brays manor house in the square moat is said to have been superseded by another nearer the road, and this, by then an old timber-framed house, is believed to have been destroyed by fire in the first half of the nineteenth century. A recent investigator of the present Worts farmhouse showed a substantial timber-framed house whose roof, under the additions of the nineteenth century, had been entirely replaced. Much of the first manor house of Brays outside the moat may be embodied in the present house. The roof may have been the main casualty of the fire. The area between the house and the road is full of suggestive earthworks, which may well represent good candidates for investigation. Old stacks and clamps, even the spoil from cleaning the pond, may have laid false trails.

The site of the Chamberlains manor house (or, in the stilted legal language of the time, capital messuage), remains now as the centre of a very extensive and complex system of moats, this corner of the village being the lowest, closest to the fens, and most exposed to floods. Defence,

8 The north face of Worts Farm. The plastered walls belong to a very much earlier house, of three rooms up- and three downstairs, which must have been a manor house of Brays after the moated site was abandoned.

45

9 The tapping drain that runs across the north end of the Green, constructed to divert water away from the site of the manor of Chamberlains.

drainage and navigation (barge traffic), all played their part in the design, and separate, but inside the complex, is the old mediaeval fish pond. There is a ditch running across the north end of the Green, partly filled in where the road runs through, obviously constructed as a 'tapping drain' to collect the water coming out of the slightly sloping ground on the west. The ditch passes between banks erected against flood and joins the canals in the east. Broad moats, in some places double, show the platform of the manor house as far as the churchyard boundary. Modern extensions of the churchyard have encroached upon the manor site, and in that part the graves contain much mediaeval pottery, some of it probably from the villagers of the Domesday Survey. The last mention that I have found of the manorial 'watergate' was in 1367, and this was probably east of the church and manor house, near the present old tithe barn. It was mentioned in connection with an obstruction for which Sir Thomas de Eltisley was responsible. He was the Master of Corpus Christi College, Cambridge, still involved in the long-drawn out processes of purchasing the manor of Landbeach from the Chamberlains.

5

High Farming

In face of the demand for food for the increasing population, and the consequent opportunity to profit from rising prices, the old type of manorial administration responded. Lords once again began to favour keeping their demesne lands in their own hands, and cultivating them mainly by labour from villein rents, buying in extra or specialist services only as necessary. These were directed by villein officers, chosen in the manor court, according to known custom, overseen and checked by the steward at the annual audit and monthly courts. Because the system at its most effective involved the use of written record, and because the new lord of the manor, Corpus Christi College, was literate to the point of hoarding records, enough information survives for us to glimpse mediaeval high farming at Landbeach.

For instance, the peasant's farming year is outlined by the detailed seasonal variations in the obligations to labour for the lord. The 164 week-works due from each of the greater customers (the five-acre men of earlier documents) were very closely defined:

From Michaelmas (29th September) to Gules (1st) of August, 43 weeks and five days each year, three works each week on Monday, Tuesday and Wednesday.

From 1st August to Michaelmas, eight weeks and three days each year, four works each week on Monday, Tuesday, Wednesday and Friday.

From Michaelmas to Christmas a ploughing work every Friday.

He and his fellows must mow the lord's meadow whensoever it was ready for mowing and gathering. On these occasions he would have as much grass as he could reasonably carry on the handle of his scythe, and if the handle broke he should have none. He and his partners should have four acres of mowing meadow, two-and-a-half in the moor and one-and-a-half in the meadow between Landbeach and Waterbeach.

Between 1st August and Michaelmas he and his fellows must cut and carry the lord's corn four days in the week, on Monday, Tuesday, Wednesday and Friday (worth ¾d. a day without food). Each week in harvest he must provide a boon-work (i.e. a free day's work) with two men (in practice the wife could go, but on some Ely manors she was excepted), the lord providing food, i.e. at each bedrepe (boon-work) two loaves, one at noon and one at night, of whole flour as it came from the mill, where 24 loaves made six quarterns, and also four herrings, two at noon and two at night.

And if reaping was not needed for the corn, then he should reap the straw at the will of the lord, and the lord would allow it to count as a work. On every day on which he mowed straw he would again be entitled to as much as he could reasonably carry on the snaithe (handle) of his scythe.

Every week in the year he had to perform a carrying work as often and to whatsoever place in the shire that the lord wished to send him with his fellows, to the furthest part of Cambridgeshire without food or expenses. If he did carrying work outside the county the lord should provide all reasonable costs and expenses. For each carrying work he was to take two bushels of wheat, three bushels of barley or dredge corn, half a quarter or four bushels of oats, or all other necessaries that he could reasonably cart or carry on horses.

He was to perform winter or summer works in due season: namely, he should thresh, ditch, dig the garden and peat, and all other honest and reasonable manual works, and in addition he was to stack turf, and when he did so should have five turves for his own fire. He was to make and deliver three quarters of malt by full measure at his own costs, but if the lord did not want the malt he made, then he would get nothing for it. He was to find a stack for the lord, as did his fellows each year.

When he died, a heriot was due to the lord, and further, his youngest son should give a heriot at the will of the lord if he wished to take over the tenement of his father. (The heriot was a death duty owed to the lord on the death of a villein, the villein's best beast at the lord's choice.) If he should be summoned before the justices, coroners or other ministers of the Lord King, he should be excused one work if it happened on a work day. If he should row the lord, lady or their sons to Ely, Wisbech or elsewhere, the lord or lady should find him and his partners his food. If he should row to fetch and carry corn or other necessaries to and from Wisbech in taking the bailiff or attorney of the lord and lady, he should, again, have food.

This represents what must have been about the limit the villein could bear. The extras were demanded at precisely the times when the peasant

needed to give maximum attention to his own holding, at sowing and harvest. He needed able-bodied children living at home, or he would have to hire help. Even the double heriot suggests a sort of rack-renting. Normally one heriot was due to the lord on the death of a villein; to exact a second from the heir seems oppressive. Inheritance by the younger son, a custom known as Borough English, was common in this area, and is usually thought of as a defence against the worst poverty; but if it is so here, it is not at the lord's cost.

The minor customers, with only half a standard villein holding, performed similar services to those of their major brethren, except that they did not plough. Instead they mowed, carried and reaped, on meadow, corn and stubble, three times a week, Monday, Tuesday and Friday, from 1st August to St Andrew's Day (30th November).

Those with very tiny holdings indeed, the successors to the coterells of the Hundred Rolls, and possibly to the cottars and bordars of Domesday itself, paid boon-works, but were exempt from week-works. Thus they formed a labour reserve when most needed. They may have been better off than many of their apparently more substantial fellows, for by this time the common lawyers were interpreting liability to week-work as a test of unfreedom. They had time and opportunity to make a living and raise a shilling a year for rent, and a little more for other dues. The man at the end of the list, perhaps in some sense at the bottom of the

49

heap, rejoices in the name Littlemagge (or possibly Littlewagge). He has no other name. He could scarcely need it with that name that grins at us through the ages like the green man in the church roof. He held a cottage and half an acre, but he may in fact have been free with no week-work. If so the sheriff would listen to him in court when he would send major customers back to their own lord in his manor court.

Having looked at the labour services from the point of view of the peasantry who suffered them, it may be worthwhile to examine them as part of the working of a productive enterprise.

The first deductions from the theoretical total of works available were for the reeve who was excused the whole of his 164 works for a year in office. The manor court also chose such other officers as were necessary and customary: haywards, represents, swineherds, supervisors of the fields and of the drains. (The represve's job was to 'bear a rod over the backs of the workers to encourage them to work diligently'.) The word in the record is *elected* or *chosen* according to how the Latin is read. The jury was elected in Landbeach, and there appears never to have been a fixed rotation around the houses as in some other places. But the jurors seemed to know whose turn it was, and at the level of simple manor courts at this period election amounts to a declaration of right in the matter of office-holding.

When such lesser officers were otherwise engaged on duty they also were excused the appropriate number of works.

The account rolls, where they exist in good condition, enable us to see the villein as manager in action, in the person of the reeve.

In the Black Death year we can see Richard Pelle, in spite of sickness, coping with the use of the available labour services:

Ploughing works in the four seasons	292
Muck spreading	32
Breaking up a tilth for spring sowing	30
Two pieces of wall new-built around the court	8
Enclosing private ground around the manor	6
Helping dig the land for sowing flax and hemp and in lifting the same linen and hemp	12
Bundling and stacking straw	85
Mowing grass in the Frith Fen	32
Turning, lifting and helping (i.e. hay-making)	24
Reaping the lord's corn	61
Allowed to several customary tenants this year on account of their infirmity because of the Pestilence	24
Sowing the lord's corn, reaping, binding and helping, drying in shocks and turning from time to time	904
Sold	181

As well as the 164 works excused from Richard because of his office, no less than 452 were lost because peasant tenements fell into the lord's hand. This reflects the Pestilence, as do the 24 days sick. Henry Gardener, Thomas Richards and William the Miller died and their lands came into the lord's hands, with crops growing on them; this might have helped out in this difficult year if there were enough to harvest.

The labour services of the villeins could not cope with some of the more specialised jobs about the manor, and probably never could. Richard Pelle took on a couple of sets of ploughmen, two holders for ten weeks, and two drivers for ten weeks and three days. The mediaeval plough needed two men, the holder grasping the handles and steering, while the driver kept the team pulling. He also took on a cowman for ten

Fig. 6 Landbeach: open fields and the water table. The open arable fields of the village as they developed under pressure of flooding from the fens in the fourteenth century.

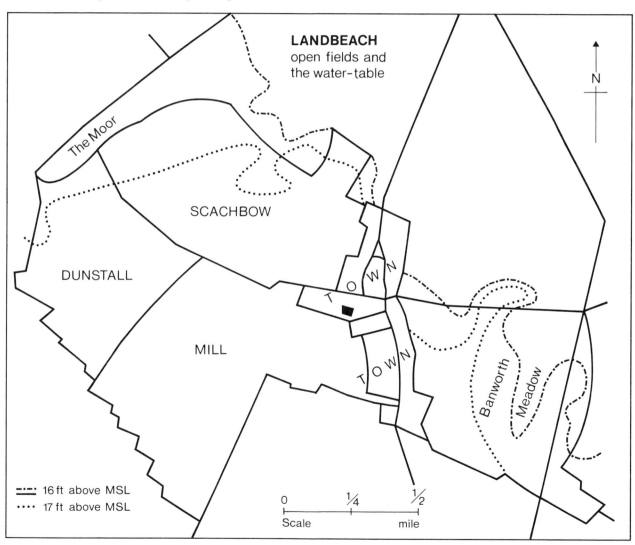

weeks, as well as Walter Wragg and Henry Lowedman for ten weeks on unspecified duties. A shepherd was employed between Michaelmas and Martinmas for six weeks. The 'work sold' item is always the number of works owed but not called on, since the lord always had the option of taking cash instead of work. Thus, from year to year, the lord could exercise whatever degree of commutation of works into cash he chose, without changing irrevocably. The work of the villein reeve as managing director of a sizeable enterprise is most impressive.

At the annual audit, every change in stock during the whole year was accounted for. No less than twenty-four separate headings were used for livestock. Capons, for example, began the year with 19 received in customary rents. Chevage fees (payments by villeins for permission to live outside the manor) added another three. In the debit were five killed by 'le PolKat' that was later caught. A total of 38 went in entertainment, and five to a man for singing in front of the children, by the gift of the lady. One can imagine this scene in the year of the Pestilence, in the damp old house in the interminable rain, and death all around outside. I hope that he sang well.

The geese produced 80 eggs; the hens nothing because they had been rented out at 1d. a dozen hens, and so 460 eggs were bought in. The dovecotes produced 445 pigeons, all of which went in hospitality (literally house-keeping).

Foreign expenses, i.e. those incurred off the manor, on several occasions show cloth for gowns for the lord, lady and boys, and also commons for the boys at school (university).

Similar charges, credit and debit, purchases and sales are all recorded with great exactness. Strays and heriots as well as live births add to the income. Malt was made and sold. With the hens all out on hire, as the pullets produced a few small eggs these were sold off at 1d. for twenty, only the best quality being acceptable on the manor table. Ten cows were let out at full farm (i.e. for the whole year), and four at half farm. The full rate was 5s.8d. a cow. The peasant could cope with the labour-intensive dairying, while the lord had the capital for breeding and marketing. Items like sale of fruit from the lord's garden, and sale of stubble, all helped swell the total. But the biggest source of non-agricultural income, even surpassing the enhanced rent from leasing more demesne, were the perquisites of court, the profits of justice, fines from the customary court.

Among the petty expenses are items in which the manor could not be self-sufficient. The smith was paid for repairs to all the iron fittings on the ploughs, gates, houses, mill and other buildings, carthouse, etc. Parchment for the rolls was a regular if tiny item, hospitality for the staff at the courts and audit, a regular and large amount.

11 Mediaeval timber-work still survives in the Plague House.

Whenever building repairs were in progress, great quantities of nails always seemed to be provided. The carpentry of the time seems heavily dependent on them, and this helps to explain the quantities of deeply corroded nails that turned up on the mediaeval house sites in the village, far more than other types of find.

The most valuable lands on the manor were eleven doles of mowing meadow in the Moor, worth 52s. for 26 acres. There were another six, but these were worn out and worth only 4s.9d.—12d. an acre on four acres and three roods (i.e. half price). Between Landbeach and Waterbeach, in

53

the area known later as Hardmede or Fortmade, were 28 doles containing 45 acres and three roods, making an annual total of mowing meadow of 75 acres and three roods belonging to the Chamberlains demesnes.

Even in an area richly endowed with lush grassland, like Landbeach on the fen edge, we picture country life in the Middle Ages as revolving around the cultivation of the arable, with the ox team pulling the heavy plough, and all the works following in due season: making tilth, sowing, harrowing, reaping, and thrashing in the barn in winter. None of the documents shows this more than the Domesday Book itself. In its summary of each manor the central questions are the possible extent of its arable, and the actual amount being cultivated: how many ploughs there are and how many there might be. The details of meadow are recorded much more erratically.

In organising the cultivation of what today would be quite a substantial farm, the reeve was guided by custom. The customary rate of sowing was per acre:

3   bushels of wheat
4½   ,,   ,, barley
5   ,,   ,, dredge corn (or drage, a mixture of oats and barley)
6   ,,   ,, oats
4   ,,   ,, beans
3   ,,   ,, peas

The amount could be reduced on land cropped the year before and due for fallowing the next year.

The actual rotations of the three seasons, as in other nearby villages, had, by the early fourteenth century, developed a flexibility which might well be lost in a later period. The Chamberlains cropping in Black Death year makes good sense:

Spring Season—Dunstall field	Drage and a little oats
Winter—Mill Field	Wheat and maslin (rye and wheat mixed)
	Barley
Fallow—Scachbow and Banworth	Beans, black and green peas, vetches
	All these in the fallow are leguminous.

A few more oats were grown in the meadow. Two shillings were paid for bringing oats from Wisbech, purchased by the lord.

Hemp and flax were raised in the courtyard.

Oats could be sown latest of the grains, and were more tolerant of wet, cold land. But they were erratic cropping, and not grown much except where they were needed for horses. In this year heriots, strays and the rector's legacy had inflated the total of horses of all kinds to 15, and in consequence oats seem particularly in demand.

During the year, two bushels of wheat were given to the nunnery of St Radegund and 23 quarters one bushel went to housekeeping; six quarters of maslin went to housekeeping and one quarter in alms. A peck of green peas went to the kitchen and for housekeeping expenses. A further 13 quarters and six bushels of wheat went to the digging of 30,000 turves, payment in grain.

In this part of the country the agricultural techniques in use by manorial lords who were cultivating their land by villein reeve and villein labour force, were probably at their peak in the first half of the fourteenth century. The elimination of much of the bare fallow by sowing leguminous crops fed the soil as well as both humans and livestock. Any improvement in productivity was as likely to go on charity and lavish entertainment as productive investment, but the achievement was not unimpressive, even if it did not beat inflation.

6

When the Rains Came

The deterioration of the climate in the fourteenth century probably affected the fenland and the fen edge more than anywhere else in the country. Not only was 1316 the first year of the great famine, but also a year of unprecedented rainfall. Places that had never been flooded before were reported flooded. The effect of all this changed the field system of Landbeach. It is most fortunate for us that it is for this year that the very detailed Extent (or Survey) of the lands of Agnes de Bray survives.

In this document plot after plot in the lower-lying parts of the arable, but not the higher parts, is designated, 'and is common unless sown'. The distribution makes it clear that these were areas affected by flooding.

Before these woes had been overcome, disease struck the flocks and herds. The court rolls of 1328 reveal peasant flocks of a size unlikely to be sustained. John Haldeyn committed trespass with 300 in the pasture, John Sweyn with 200 in the Frith Fen, and Henry Sandre in the lady's peas with 100.

The reeve's accounts for 1349 show no sheep in the list of the lord's beasts. Peasant flocks are revealed mainly in trespass cases and cases of failure to put all sheep in the seigneurial fold, a privilege valued by lords of manors. These reveal peasant flocks increasing for a number of years, and then suddenly being wiped out by 'murrain', a term which seems to cover all ills of mediaeval sheep. The counterpart to the ups and downs of the sheep population in fourteenth century Landbeach are the herds of mares and foals that come in to replace the sheep and trespass in their stead. For example, at a court in 1372 there were 51 cases of trespass involving 105 horses, only one cow and no sheep at all.

The great flooding and the disease of the farm animals were followed by what was probably the worst natural catastrophe to strike these islands in recorded history—the Pestilence as all the contemporary documents called it, although it is enshrined in popular memory as the Black Death. In 1349 it swept through Landbeach and adjoining villages. In the Chamberlains account rolls, the stock account includes ten heriots—there had been twenty peasant tenements on the Chamberlains manor that were liable for heriot. The parson died as well, leaving three beasts to the lord.

After the shock of the Pestilence, we can glimpse a little of the aftermath. In 1350 an investigation was ordered to list the names of all those who had appropriated and carried away window shutters, doors and other timber from divers houses currently in the lord's hand. For a moment there is a glimpse of a half-ghost village, with looting where the plague had passed on. The court rolls tell more. Walls and fences had become ruinous from failure to make essential repairs. Animals were straying in the hay and growing corn. Bands of villeins failed to turn up for their harvest works. The lord did not find it possible to replace all his dead villein landholders with men prepared to accept the old conditions. Five tenements were let for life at a small cash rent with an obligation to provide one man for one day in hay harvest for lifting the crop. This was practically giving the land for nothing compared with the heavy labour services under the pre-plague terms. Too much had been lost through failure to cope with getting the harvest home to miss even one man's work for a single day. In any case, he was taking land that no one seemed to want.

Of nine cattle caught wandering and impounded as strays, not one was claimed.

Leases changed, and the main clauses of many were the obligation to inhabit and maintain the tenement. Desperate times called for desperate remedies. Peasants helped themselves to the lord's corn and turf for sale. At one court in 1356, nine peasants were presented for stealing the lord's corn and a further 32 for trespass in the lord's crops. By 1357 things were getting even more out of hand. John Emme went out into the fen by night, stealing the turves of several of his neighbours to sell in Cambridge. A woman and her daughter raided a villein's house for timber. Stealing from the lord had been one thing, although before the Pestilence it was not frequent, and stealing from fellow villagers very rare. Now the villeins seem to have learnt the habit of looting, and are prepared to steal from their fellows quite flagrantly.

John Vaude broke into a close of Martyn the Smith and stole his goose. John Martyn was one of those whose turves had been taken from the fen and disposed of in Cambridge market. John Sandre broke the pale of the lord's pound and a lock on the park wall. Matilda Heyward carried off

12 The heart of the village, looking south. In the centre is the piece of land described in 1459 as 'like a tongue stuck out towards the north'. The square moat of the manor of Brays is hidden in the trees in the upper right-hand corner. The church spire can be seen towards the centre, and the light, square field shows some of the moats of the manor of Chamberlains. The double ditch and banks of the fourteenth-century flood defences are very clear in the lower half of the picture, and the clump of trees just above these conceals the mediaeval fish pond. *Cambridge University Collection: copyright reserved.*

sheaves of dredge corn belonging to John Knyght and others contrary to the lord's peace, and carried off herbage of divers men contrary to the lord's peace, etc.

In 1361 timber was carried off, the lord's fence broken, and apples were stolen from his garden. Agnes Knyth, who had farmed the manor, was presented for waste and damage in walls and fences with her animals, especially letting her male animals roam all over the village. After warning she was fined 100s. Her farming of the manor may not have been quite as grand as it sounds, being possibly of only one empty holding. She seems, along with John Emme, to have died without heirs in 1361. The village was probably suffering from the Second Pestilence. She seems to have left a trail of neglect.

It is hard to connect many disorderly acts directly to the aftermath of the Black Death, but the worst in the area seems to have happened at Denney Abbey, a mere hundred yards across the boundary in the north end of the parish. This was in 1350. The Chancery writ tells most of the story:

> . . . that Thomas de Lexham, clerk, and divers other malefactors and disturbers of the Peace of the lord King, within the Festival of the Nativity of St John the Baptist, in the regnal year of the King that now is, the 24th, at the house of the enclosed Sisters of Denney in the said County of Cambridge, cut through the fences, and intended to take and abduct certain of the nuns themselves, contrary to the Form of Protection of the lord King . . .

13 Much clunch has been used at the north end of the village, probably robbed from the ruins of the abandoned manor house of Chamberlains. Here it forms a garden wall, and appears to have been re-used.

His name, de Lexham, suggests that he was a Norfolk man, certainly not a local; he was probably one of those priests who had deserted their posts in the epidemic, and had taken to vagrancy and crime. Similar bad characters infested the countryside for the next generation, and many survived to play a part in the Peasants' Revolt in 1380.

In 1365 the most dramatic change in the manor of Chamberlains began. The demesne arable, all two hundred and six acres of it, was let to sixteen villeins in varying amounts for thirteen years at 18d. an acre, but offences in the court rolls continued much as before. In the following year twenty-one cases of over-digging turf were punished by seizing the turf and fining the diggers. There were twenty-seven cases of damage in the Meadow, the Frith Fen, and in the peas and corn, etc. The bedell had failed to collect the fines of the previous court as he should. Bringing in of 'foreign' beasts for pasture for payment began to run into a serious problem of overstocking. Illegal pasturing of animals from outside, and trespasses by foreigners in the village pastures and corn became more frequent and serious. The law was flagrantly flouted and broken by those who came from across the parish boundary. The manor court was not designed to cope with the worst of such cases, and it seems almost a matter for surprise if an offender from another village calls in to the court to pay his fine and make peace. After the Second Pestilence the court seemed no longer able to exercise such close control as before. But all was not yet lost for the lord, nor gained for the villeins. They were not yet free.

Some of the old disabilities of villeinage were beginning to soften. In practice it was becoming harder to prevent a villein from leaving the manor. After the Second Pestilence flight becomes more frequent as the chances of escape seem to improve. In the old days, the need of a licence from the lord to marry a villein daughter had enabled the lord to charge what the traffic would bear; in the last quarter of the fourteenth century it would no longer bear very much.

But the prospects must have seemed good for the lord if he bided his time. He might, taking his opportunities as they came, recover much of the *de facto* power which was still legally his. The bedell would not always fail to distrain a peasant's chattels for the payment of a fine. The lords in Landbeach could still claim the performance of customary works rather than sell them. As late as 1367 two villeins were sold by the lord of the manor of Chamberlains, Corpus Christi College, along with their lands and all their children, 'both now and in the future'. Many of the fourteen men who had failed to do their harvest works in 1349 were dead. Those who refused their works in 1380 were very much alive.

In that year we get no direct evidence of Landbeach men joining the revolt which raged around the area, but something seems to have been afoot. Order had to be given to seize John Sandre, Thomas Sandre and John Emme, the lord's villeins who had fled the manor without licence. Three pieces of demesne land that had been illegally occupied without permission were discovered and seized back for the lord. The other charges—rent arrears, 21 trespasses in the lord's crops, 16 stopped watercourses, three of over-digging turf to the extent of 1,000, 6,000 and 6,000, and two of breaches of the bye-laws about mowing grass—might have come to any court. If anything, there seems to have been less in the way of disputes between peasant and lord, and more between peasant and peasant.

But it is in 1380 that we get the most serious case of theft in the rolls: John Bernard accused Thomas Michel of stealing six ewes out of his yard. At the Bartholomew court no less than 118 cases of trespass were listed.

A new formula appears in the rolls for 1380: instead of recording, 'X did trespass in (place) with (so many) (kind of animal)', a phrase which suggests more violence in local government becomes general: 'was taken with . . . in . . .'

Thomas the sheep stealer had other nocturnal occupations: sending his pigs by night outside of his yard into the lord's corn!

The effect of the great Peasants' Revolt in 1380 may have been merely to leave the landlords more firmly in the saddle for the time being. None of our evidence suggests that Landbeach men were directly involved, but the village is situated only a few miles from Cambridge on the direct route to Ely, both of which had very serious outbreaks of violence. In the next village, Cottenham, the mob from Cambridge arrived to attack the Harleston Manor house, property of one of the tax collectors.

And the lord of the manor of Chamberlains, Corpus Christi College, was attacked by the townsmen, even though it was the townsmens' college, having been founded by town guilds. The reason for this apparently strange behaviour is that its patron was none other than the most hated man in the country, the Duke of Lancaster, John of Gaunt.

While some of his fellow clerics were down the road to Cambridge playing somewhat ambiguous parts in the Peasants' Revolt, the Vicar of Waterbeach had all his sheep repeatedly in the lord's oats in Landbeach. In East Anglia, including Cambridgeshire, the Revolt was put down without scruple, but the peasants do not seem to have been cowed. In 1383 Roger Sandre, John Martyn, John Fen, John Sweyn, Roger Wylmyn, John Symme and John Herne, all villeins, failed to report for carrying service at Cambridge on the Saturday before Epiphany, but were rebellious against the custom of the manor and the lord's brewer. But who would want to do carrying service, carrying corn, on Old Christmas Day?

Henry Marot, a poor old cottager, could no longer cope. The house was ruinous, and he had neither strength nor money to pay for repairs. The jury was ordered to elect one of their number to take the holding on the old customary terms, but they refused and were declared 'tepid and negligent'. So the land was freed and the whole homage became collectively responsible for the customary works and dues belonging to it. Close on the heels of the Peasants' Revolt, this was a drastic piece of estate management, but nearby manors were doing the same thing. Compulsion was becoming more and more obvious in relations between lord and peasant. But the consequences of the fall in population at the time of the Pestilence meant that whatever the law, the peasant could in fact often bargain with the lord, where he disliked custom. Slowly, uncertainly and with many reverses, bargain replaced custom and the villein drifted to freedom.

The poverty of many of the lesser clergy, which helped to provide some of the middle leadership in the Peasants' Revolt, had its reflection in Landbeach. Thomas the chaplain, servant to the parson, was caught house-breaking at John Amable's, a villein's, and struck him 'contrary to peace'. The whole period could be called contrary to peace.

The abandonment of the cultivation of the demesne land and the letting of it to a farmer seems to have begun before the College's purchase of the manor was complete. That was not achieved until 1369, at the end of a chain of transactions lasting ten years. But in 1361, when Agnes Knyth died without heirs, she is called 'farmer of the manor this past year'. In 1365, as mentioned previously, what appears to have been the first of a series of thirteen-year leases was concluded. All the demesne land, certainly all the arable, was let to sixteen villeins in various parcels. We have less information about the manor of Brays, but by 1401 at least they had a farmer (lessee), and their court rolls show that it was proving difficult to control him and prevent short-term exploitation at the long-term cost of neglect and dilapidation of buildings and land. There was precisely the same trouble on Brays manor from the bailiff's letting the sheepfold instead of using it to build up the fertility of the lord's land.

By 1384 there were marked signs that the landlord was losing control, not only to the farmer, but also to the peasants. At the court on the Feast of St Faith, Virgin, there were trespasses reported by four hundred and eighty sheep, owned by four peasants, and five hundred and fourteen sheep left outside the lord's fold.

Before the end of the century the lords of Brays were back in residence again and, early in the next, they were asserting their rights over the hollow-way from their moated manor house as a church path for the lords, their families and tenants, servants and ministers.

Within a few years of the purchase of the manor of Chamberlains by Corpus Christi, it became customary to appoint either the Master or a Senior Fellow as rector, a useful form of outdoor relief for senior members. A notable exception was Master Adam Clerke who held the living from 1429–1462. But connections with the College as lord were always so close as to have something of the effect of a permanently resident landlord.

Adam Clerke was a farming parson, in our sense of the term, with a vengeance. Neither Master nor Fellow, he was a friend and executor of one of the great Masters, Richard Billingford. He was resident in the Rectory, one of two big houses in the village, and active in cultivating the glebe along with extra land leased from the College, as well as in collecting his tithes. His reign in the village foreshadows the squire-parsons of later centuries. It was under the mastership of Billingford (whose image is preserved in a brass in St Benet's Church, at that time serving as College chapel), that he was able to lease the largest addition to the manor. This was a property which kept the title of its former owner, Bradfields. It was a group of buildings, paddocks and yards around the heart of the manorial barns and other farm-buildings. North of the manor house and churchyard was hallyard and sheepen, and the home pastures Meadow Croft, or Maidcroft, and Shepherds Croft. Across the road was (and is) a garden which was claimed by rectors much later as Rectory Glebe. Now an adventure playground, it is still perfectly recognisable from its description in a rental of 1459, and mentioned in

14 The Rectory as it appears today, developed from the house inhabited by Adam Clerke in the fifteenth century. The symmetrical façade was created by Robert Masters in the eighteenth century, and the stone porch was added by John Tinkler.

less detail a hundred years before that. The rental describes it thus: '. . . in shape and bodily form triangular, within and without the garden (of the rector), in shape like an oblong tongue stuck out towards the north.' Elsewhere it mentions a pond there, and it is still there, breeding rare species, like crested newts. At the same time Master Adam was allowed to have his own pound, Parson's Pinfold, for impounding stray animals.

It was in his first year as rector that the College leased the manor to eight of their customary tenants, as we saw above. In 1440 a similar lease for twelve years was made to Master Adam for him to divide the demesnes among individual tenants. The rent was ninepence per acre. The complicated clause about rent in the 1429 lease was dropped. This had fixed the rent at eightpence if the peasants were willing to take it for twelve years. Otherwise they must take it for nine years at eightpence halfpenny. The next lease was in 1454. Perhaps Master Adam was feeling that the time had come to take things more easily. The manor was in that year leased to three peasants for twelve years simply at ninepence per acre. The leases all mention pasture or meadows and fen in vague general terms, and there are separate leases for some of the permanent enclosed pastures like Moorlees and Scachbowlees. There is more than a hint of the separation of grazing rights from arable and grass, and even in Landbeach, where there would have been plenty left, such acts were regarded as anti-social.

About the time that the twelve-year lease of 1454 ran out, the two Talbot sisters, Elizabeth, Dowager Duchess of Norfolk, and Eleanor, widow of Sir Thomas Boteler, became interested in the College. Some of the money they provided was used to purchase sheep 'to be at Beach for the weal of the College'. The sheep stock were wiped out by disease when William Sowode was rector, but the manor was soon restocked by Matthew Parker's time as rector of Landbeach, 1545–1554. Parker seems to have used an elaborate scheme of leases to his wife and half-brother, John Baker, to provide what looks like a marriage allowance, since he was the first married incumbent at Landbeach. Baker surrendered the lease halfway through its course to provide twenty scholarships to the College, and an equal amount for the Master.

1. The Parish Church of All Saints, Landbeach. Recent discoveries during restoration indicate a Norman origin. *Photo: Richard Muir*

2. (*above*) The mediaeval fish pond of the manor of Chamberlains. *Photo: Richard Muir*

3. (*left*) Here the cornfields still come down to the High Street, recalling the open field system of mediaeval times. *Photo: Jack Ravensdale*

4. (*opposite above*) The hollow-way through what is now a recreation ground disappeared when the field was levelled. It was claimed in 1415 as a right of way to church for all the people of the manor of Brays. There were three peasant tenements on either side of the way that have gone to make the field. *Photo: Jack Ravensdale*

5. (*opposite below*) The clump of trees hides the manor of Brays moated site. Ancient earthworks in the foreground are revealed by the buttercups. *Photo: Jack Ravensdale*

6. (*above*) The old common from Waterbeach Road, lost to the villagers at the Enclosure of 1813. The Rectory is in front of the church and the Tithe Barn on the right. *Photo: Richard Muir*

7. (*left*) The East window of the parish church is made from fragments of glass from various ages, mostly brought by Robert Masters from Wimborne Minster in Dorset. The central figure is reputed to be the Lady Margaret Beaufort, with her parents, grandparents of Henry VII, on either side. *Photo: Richard Muir*

7

Copyholders and Gentlemen

The drift of the peasantry towards freedom continued by fits and starts. With hindsight it appears inexorable. At the time, fortune seemed fickle. Gradually the customary tenements or bondage holdings of the villeins turned into copyhold—customary tenure, proved by copy of the court roll, with labour services replaced by cash rents, usually fixed by custom, and all taint of personal unfreedom gone. Where custom had fixed the cash rent the inflations of the sixteenth century would reduce its value until it remained a mere nuisance and the peasants felt themselves full owners. Heriot often remained, but as a slighter nuisance.

The fitfulness of the process was clear in Landbeach. Among the Chamberlains archives is a list from as early as 1352 in which rents are given entirely as cash, and the amounts due for rented land and the amounts for commuted works are carefully distinguished and tabulated as quarterly payments. The whole of the lord's arable was being let out in parcels to his own villeins. This was in the last years of the Chamberlain regime, before they sold to the College. It followed hard on the heels of the great Pestilence, a very early example of a lord responding to that disaster by giving up cultivation, with all the problems of a desperate labour shortage, and attempting to live from rents. The new compound holdings were larger than they had been in the Hundred Rolls, and probably far greater than at Domesday.

But in 1361 there is still a list of works owed—thirty-seven of them— and further, a list of cottagers that the jury declares owe two works each week, and that each of them pays instead of works 6s.8d. A tenant with twenty acres gives the lord ten shillings for ten acres, and for the other ten does three works each week.

There is a surprising flexibility which, exploited for the benefit of the lord, eventually played into the peasant's hands.

After the Chamberlains, with the lord being a Cambridge college, this flexibility went even further. The villeins whose works had been commuted could seek to earn cash for their rents by looking for work with their lord in the city as well as in the village. An expense list from the late fifteenth century indicates how convenient these odd jobs could be for both sides, and incidentally reveals a slightly Falstaffian quality about the subsistence in Cambridge:

Expenses and payments made and paid in the seventh year of King Edward the fourth (1467–8)

Includes:

Parson, for twenty loads of straw	13s.4d.
Making of walls for barn	20s.0d.
Pery Chirche for six days' work in coping the lordship walls	2s.0d.
Henry Garard 1½ days' work at pinfold	6d.
William Sweyn one day's work at pinfold	4d.
Simon Herne six days at the coping of the wall	2d.
13 cartfuls of hay	13d.
Simon Herne for carriage of two loads of straw to the north barn	4d.
Same Simon half day hire of his horse for to draw water	
John Fen for fetching a load of sedge	4d.
At the court for bread	6d.
6 gallons of ale	1½d.
Beef, mutton and pork	14d.
In Cambridge ale, 1 gallon	
a goose	5d.
a capon	4d.
for pepper, saffron, and powder of cinnamon	1d.
for mustard and salt	1d.
for the wife's labour and for washing of clothes	3d.
for fuel	4d.
in horsemeat	4d.

Other works are not specified.

When this kind of commercial piecemeal arrangement began to displace the old compulsory labour-rents, villeinage was near its end, but the end finally came when the Royal Prerogative courts, followed by the Common Law Courts, refused to entertain any plea of unfreedom against any native-born Englishman.

*   *   *

Without doubt the most distinguished and famous of all our rectors was Matthew Parker. When Queen Elizabeth I came to the throne she needed a new Archbishop of Canterbury; Cardinal Pole, Catholic Mary's last Archbishop, had conveniently died on the same day as his royal mistress and so avoided the worst kind of embarrassment. Parker had not left the country as most of his friends had during Mary's persecutions, but had survived by keeping on the move around Norfolk. It had done his nerves no good, and he was in any case a nervous man who was enough of a hypochondriac to have obtained permission to wear a hat when preaching for fear of colds in the head. His last benefice before the elevation to Canterbury was the rectory of Landbeach. As Master of Corpus Christi he devoted very considerable effort to gathering together all the Anglo-Saxon documents that he could lay his hands on from the dispersed libraries of dissolved religious houses, and these now make the Parker Library in the College, one of the very richest for such material. Possibly his greatest triumph was in rescuing and preserving a Gospel Book which was either brought or sent to Augustine when he first brought Christianity from Rome.

But he did not scorn to use his talents for more mundane purposes. The College still has a mass of documents in the handwriting of Parker and his secretaries describing the estates in great detail. For Landbeach he produced a field book of the conventional kind, listing the size, past and present ownership and occupation of every scrap of land in the village. There is also a tabular version, with his own code of symbols, signed by him, which can give a simultaneous oversight of the whole. What would he have done with a computer! But more than all, this timid man defended his village tenants in Landbeach against a violent gang of oppressors led by Richard Kirby, lord of the manor of Brays, who was apparently going insane. Parker probably needed the Rectory of Landbeach as he was one of the first generation of married priests after the Reformation. He was later to survive Queen Elizabeth's tongue. An encounter with her is the occasion of the most well-known story about him, when, at the end of a stay with the Parkers at Lambeth Palace, the Queen's final words to Mrs Parker were: 'Madam I may not call you; Mistress I am ashamed to call you; so I know not what to call you; but yet I thank you.'

Among the papers formerly in the parish chest at Landbeach there is a list of all the closes in the village. It is in Matthew Parker's handwriting, and gives detailed measurements that correspond to the modern map. It is now pasted into the back board of a sixteenth century fen book, but its composition dates from the time when Parker compiled his field book in 1549, or perhaps the year before, when the Commission on Enclosures

Terrarum villę de Landbeche factu
et exaiatu collatione libroy ommiu veteru
et recentioy. et cu diligenti pambulatioe
tenentiu ibm maxime fide dignoy tempore
matthei parkes mri collegij corporis chri
Cantabrig primo octobris A° dm · 1549 ·
et a° XXX Edwardi Sexti sexto ⁖

Banworth

Quarentela prima

Pastura cott vocat maydecroft —
pastura coll vocat hallyeró in shepecote
cymiterm
Rectoria
——————— cois semita vocata gibbes lile
Tenemetu armigeri vocat copthall
tentu Richardi fote tenet p cartam
tentu armigeri bellys
balke pars poriacois vocat fenebar atq crosse villagij
tentu viri fote tz p carta p porsk
tentu coll' olim Thome coye Jacobi Jynkynson
tentu ori
cotagiu cott olim Ed. lane mr̃ n amye

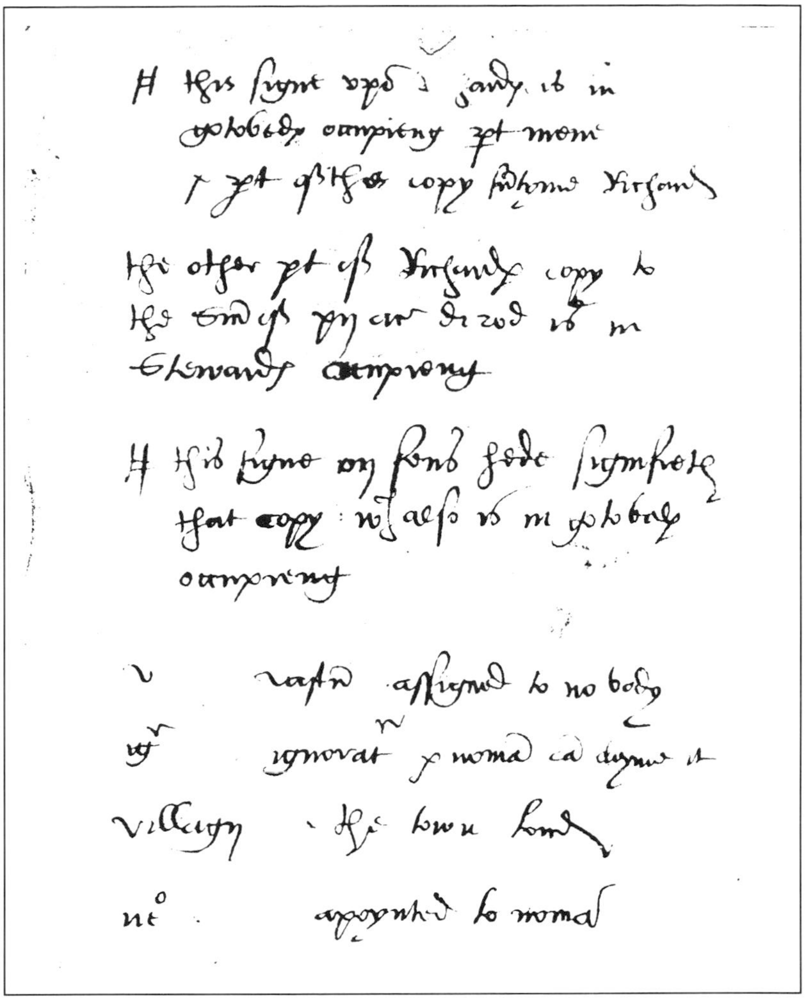

Fig. 7 (*opposite page*) The opening pages of the Field Book of 1549, parish copy. The notes are in Parker's own hand. The last cottage on the page is the author's present home.

Fig. 8 Without benefit of computer, Parker managed with symbols. Here, as so often, he writes his own programme.

of John Hales was active. It could also have been one of the preparations for supporting the case of the villagers against Richard Kirby, who briefly ran a reign of terror from his manor of Brays in that year.

Although, as mentioned earlier, the Bray family would seem to have abandoned direct cultivation soon after the great Pestilence, in favour of renting their manor, the families to whom it passed after the Brays appear to have been resident and to have become agriculturalists once more. In 1427 William Keteriche was lord, and about this time the family seem to have been connected with Denney Abbey where the Abbess was his sister.

In 1497 William Racclyffe was lord of Brays, and he was followed by one of his step-sons, Robert Kirby. They were a London family, and do not seem to have known the ways of country life. Richard, who succeeded his brother Robert in 1521, appears to have been driven by insensate greed.

At that time the country was suffering from violent inflation, but the intelligentsia of the time tended to blame everything on enclosure, which had a concrete visible form, especially the putting down of arable to grass. Much of this was going on in the Midlands, but only very little in Landbeach. Parker's list seems to have depicted a stable position with regard to enclosures and indeed the list itself may have helped to halt further inroads into the common pastures and open fields. The manor of Chamberlains had more than enough grass paddocks near at hand from the time when there had been enough tenantless land to make the Green. The manor of Brays was behind in this and Kirby had let his copyhold houses tumble in ruin until he had scarcely any copyholders left, but instead a nice clutch of empty crofts near home where he could have his ewes in the lambing season and his lambs in the winter for care and protection. These he could use as a base from which to exploit and over-stock the Landbeach fens.

The governments of Henry VIII and Edward VI, in debasing the currency, had caused the pound sterling to be heavily devalued on the continental exchanges, so producing an export boom in England's main manufacture, woollen cloth. Sheep were again to 'pay for all', as tradition said they did in England.

Landbeach had been very much a sheep village from early times. In fact, as we saw above, it probably began as a seasonal station for sheep from Waterbeach. In 1335 Henry Chamberlain, the lord of the manor, granted his brother John, the rector, the right to fold 120 sheep on strict condition that he should not have a ram. If he did Henry would have the right to destroy the fold.

Mediaeval sheep were often established on wet lands, and Landbeach, with its fens to the north, was naturally drawn into the raising of large flocks. In this peasants as well as lords played a great part. For instance, in 1366 Alan Wylmyn, son of Henry Wylmyn, together with his sister Margaret, had deserted the manor and gone off to Dry Drayton, leaving all Alan's goods in the hands of their brother Roger. The list of his goods seized by the lord showed him, although a fleeing peasant, to be a man of some substance as a sheep farmer. He had left behind him when he debunked, 44 sheep, plus 30 woolfells (skins complete with fleece), twelve lambs and two geese, as well as one-and-a-half quarters of malt and one sack. There is a profusion of cases of trespass and of failure to put sheep in the lord's fold, which reveal an enormous number of sheep in the hands of the peasants. Opportunities were therefore too great for the lords to leave exploitation of the rising prices of wool to the peasants alone.

The looms of the most highly industrialised part of the country at that

15 The hearth at 21, High Street, the author's home, a house dating from the Tudor period. A bread oven was added in the eighteenth century.

time, Norfolk and Norwich, were hastening to satisfy the last great export boom for woollen broadcloth to the continental markets: the inflation from the devaluation caused by the Great Debasement was destined to run for a few years until the calling down of the face value of the currency and the peak and collapse of the boom in 1551. In the meantime, gentlemen, yeomen, anyone who could raise sheep was drawn into the frenzied vortex. In spite of the reputation of Thomas More's *Utopia*, the causes of Kett's Rebellion were rising prices and the battle for the commons rather than enclosure, as the propaganda then current had suggested.

Although the capacity of Landbeach to produce wool was founded on its extensive fens, the distance of the fens from the built-up area and the homesteads meant that there was difficulty in supplying the extra care needed at lambing time. Richard Kirby was probably also aware of the need to bring the flocks back to higher ground should the fen stay wet. To meet this and to maximise his profits, he required home paddocks.

It was for this purpose that he allowed the houses of his copyholders to fall down, converting their crofts and tofts. He added to these ground on which he had encroached from field ways, and tried to persuade William Sowode, one of Matthew Parker's predecessors as rector and Master of the College, to exchange a number of tenements with him in order to build up a consolidated group of closes in the heart of the village, near the site of his own house. He even did a little enclosing of arable, but only 22 acres of it in all. But altogether he had tasted most of the sins of the unjust landlord in the literature of the time.

By 1548 and 1549 his harassment of the peasantry had moved on to strong-arm tactics against Chamberlains' tenants. He tried to use his power as lord to impound strays, in a move to drive the peasants from the commons. For such animals as were straying on land belonging to *his* manor, and lawfully impounded, could be regained by their owners only on payment of a sum, called a 'replevin', which the lord could fix, although it was supposed to be at a reasonable amount. Kirby could not be reasonable if he tried, and we can see very little sign of his ever trying. One of the villagers, making a statement to be used against Kirby, said, 'a froward mind and a denyless conscience he had'. He needled the peasants by impounding their oxen straight from the ploughing when they were manifestly not straying, and so held up urgent work.

Nicholas Aunger, who lived in the house in which I am now writing, had sheep impounded from the common pasture, and was charged five pence by way of replevin. Also he 'did lop five willows of the said Nicholas Aunger's which stand upon his own grounds without the licence of the said Aunger'.

The thuggery that Kirby introduced to the village life was particularly vicious against the very poor. Thomas Mytton was one such: 'the said poor man being a very poor man living of the catching of fowls'. Kirby

16 Number 21, High Street. Nicholas Aunger lived here in 1549.

impounded his mare and wore it out with work before it was returned, and after that did the same with a neat. There was an old soldier, back from the King's wars, and sick; so poor that he could not buy a mare but borrowed one from a friend. This Kirby twice impounded, taking twenty pence, a full week's wages, from the old man.

He knew how to use the law for vexation: Henry Steward and Robert Gilman were brought away from their ploughing to answer charges before the sheriff, when in fact no charges had been preferred. There is a memorandum on the back of one set of the articles against Kirby:

> Mem. The same day that Richard Kirby had my Lord Protector's letters (i.e. a summons), he rode on straight away from Cambridge to Madingley to Mr Hinde, and from Madingley to Beche, and from thence to Horningsea to one of his sons-in-law, Randall Hall, and on the day following he took his journey from Beche to Haddenham to make merry with another of his sons-in-law, to triumph abroad to defeat his appearance to My Lord's Grace, or to weary the tenants now at London, as he did mock the poor men this last term, making them to appear seven days before their day so to have tarried there whole eight or nine days from their business unless the goodness of My Lord Chancellor had not dismissed them sooner on account of their poverty.
>
> Item: He could ride from Beche to London upon one day to fetch process from the King's Bench to vex the poor men, and therefore, for any sickness or impotency, he might at this day repair up to My Lord's Grace to make his answer.
>
> Item: The said Kirby hath great confidence in his three sons-in-law which hath portionably his land in remainder after his death (i.e. they thought that his land would be divided between them on Kirby's death) of whom is reported there will be spent two or three hundred pounds in suit rather than he should sustain any lack by the said inhabitants in their enterprise against him.

He attacked not only individuals but also the whole village collectively. He refused to pay any scot and lot (the local rates of the time), but would not do his share in the watching of the beacons. He usurped the willows that the township had set and planted with the intention of reduction of rates by the sale of the annual lop of wands. These he seized along with the public path alongside them. He claimed the quit rent for the guildhall, recently built at the south end of the Green, 'as if he were the sole lord of the soil'. Eventually the two lords shared this, taking a penny each.

Kirby took in 1,200 sheep of foreigners (men living in other villages), 60 great cattle of foreigners, and 80 of his own. The villagers complained that this was running their cattle so short of feed that they were having to get relief from peasants with grass and to spare in nearby townships.

He enlarged his arable at his neighbours' expense by ploughing in the bounds and lands on either side of his own land. 'He . . . blindeth in their bounds meres and doles by his covetous dealing.' Meres were measured boundary markers in the open fields, and doles, in this sense, were field paths between strips.

But the great struggle was the battle for the commons, either common rights where the harvest of corn or hay had been taken (shack after harvest), or the permanent common of the greens and the fens. He was prepared to abuse his right of impounding to the limit, and to drive the poor men off by building up a gang of 'heavies' based upon his three sons-in-law who lived in neighbouring villages, supported by his 'un-honest hired men'. These lay in wait and ambushed the peasants with their cattle on the way to the fens. Several of the inhabitants, including at least one pregnant woman, were beaten up. When illegally enclosing a plot of common land, one of Kirby's sons-in-law stabbed a man with his sword. When the illegal impounding of the villagers' beasts was going on, Kirby himself, with sword and dagger drawn, sat at the village cross to maintain his hired men 'in their said unhonest acts'.

There seems to have been something of a climax on 7th June, 1548, when the JPs, 'having heard tell of his raging and furious behaviour', had to drop their own work to come and deal with Kirby, 'commanding him to use himself in sober manner towards God's and the King's his people, and that he should leave off his sword and weapon and walk like a man of peace, and also that he should command them of his house, and divers other servants that he had hired for the maintaining and fostering of his quarrel, that they should lie no more in wait with ironed staves and other unlawful weapons for the men of the town that should chance into the fen about their own business'. The very next day, when the JPs had gone, Kirby's gang was out again. One of the hired men carried a crabtree staff with two five-inch iron tines in it, for driving the peasants, and the others six-foot staves for driving the peasants' beasts from the fen. Directly contrary to the JPs' order, they seized numbers of cattle that were not trespassing, and impounded them, demanding quite unreasonable replevins for their release. When the peasants' wives joined them to resist Kirby's outrages, he threatened to hire more men for his mob, in greater numbers than the villagers. Approached by the constable officially with a demand that he should keep the peace, 'he answered him opprobriously, and said he would take no heed of his words'.

The inhabitants were already familiar with the words and stories of the English Bible, and they interpreted in terms of the Plagues of Egypt 'the grievous plagues and strokes of God falling from time to time in his own person, upon his corn and cattle, upon his family, perishing by the stern hand of God as may be feared'. They feared that he was attempting to drive all the tenants away so that he could enjoy all the resources of the village for himself. In spite of government opposition, such ejection of the peasant families from a village was not altogether unknown elsewhere. The reason why it did not happen in Landbeach was the intervention of Matthew Parker.

A second crisis in village affairs came on the first, second and third days of May 1549, when tenants of the Chamberlains manor faced Kirby with collective resistance. Kirby petitioned the Star Chamber, which was the appropriate court where violence was alleged. As the lawyer drafting used the stock legal phrases, he exaggerated almost to the point of parody. He listed 14 or 15 persons, 'in riotous manner arrayed, having upon them divers and sundry weapons, arrayed after the fashions and manner of war, that is to say with bills, bows, arrows, swords, daggers and other kinds of weapons'. They forcibly rounded up Kirby's cattle on the common and impounded them in Chamberlains' pound for three or four days. Kirby claimed that had he and his men resisted, 'there should have ensued some manslaughter, murder, breach of your Highness's Peace, or some other enormities which riotous persons daily use . . .' Kirby said that he and the inhabitants of his manor were 'daily put in danger of their lives, to the evil example of such-like offenders . . .'

The rejoinder seems to have been the work of Parker and his legal secretaries and, apart from the standard introduction, is restrained and has a much wider yet convincing account of Kirby's exploitation than the first rough paper of the peasants' case. The expert defence was clever enough to allege lack of strength for the defence of the realm as the result of the destruction of peasant households. It was a theme that was close to the government of the day, and would have appealed to Parker's old friends from Cambridge, then a power in government circles.

The case as prepared for the peasants' defence was all sweetness and light. The numbers involved in the violence were reduced to half a dozen. It declared that their only weapons were small rods or wands such as were normal for driving cattle.

The defence case accused Kirby of letting all his copyhold houses fall down so that the manor was reduced to only four freeholds besides his own mansion house. They excused their seizure of beasts and cattle by declaring that these had belonged to other men, and were being taken in as beasts of agistment (other men's cattle taken in for payment), so that Kirby was running 1,200 sheep from outside where his ancestors had never fed more than six or seven hundred. The six Chamberlains tenants acted, some partly in their own right and interest, and some on instructions from the lord of the manor of Chamberlains, the Master and Fellows of Corpus Christi College, Cambridge. As with so many Star Chamber cases, we have no record of the final decision. In fact the rejoinder was filed away misplaced among other papers from long before in the reign of Henry VIII. But the direct confrontation of lord and peasant seems to have ceased in Landbeach. Parker had seen such feelings out of hand on Mousehold Heath when he went to preach obedience to Kett's rebels. He was terrified to some good purpose. He seems to have put an end to violence in Landbeach by recording all the property rights definitively in the field books, fen books and similar written, legal records. In this he was working in the tradition of Domesday Book; rights and duties, whose record lay in long inviolate custom, as well as in recent agreements, were enshrined in the memory of the old men and could be made more available and permanent by taking down the verbal answers of sworn juries to questions.

What made the villagers imagine that Kirby had had a personal set of Egyptian plagues assigned divinely to him, emerges from the registers. His own and his brothers' sons were wiped out. One of the earliest entries is the birth of William, son of Raffe Kirby, on 18th October, 1538, in the middle of what looks like an influenza epidemic. He died four days later. The Gonnells lost three children in about a fortnight, but there is no sign that the villagers considered they were being punished by God.

When the manor of Brays came into Kirby's hands he had three daughters that he wished to set up in life. He seems to have done reasonably well for them. Margaret was married off to Randall Hall of Milton, the next village on the way to Cambridge. Margery he married to a farmer called William (or sometimes John) Betts of Haddenham, nearby in the other direction across the Old West River. Elizabeth married George Hasell of Huntingdon. All were substantial local farmers with an eye to the main chance.

Kirby promised as marriage settlement for each daughter the reversion of one third of the manor of Brays, plus £40 sterling, to be paid on demand. Later, Kirby claimed to have leased the third of the manor to Betts for twenty years at £30 per annum. He seemed unable to resist trying to turn even this into an opportunity for gain for himself at the expense of those whom he was supposed to be benefiting, once his schemes for stealing the commons had been frustrated.

Randall Hall, on Kirby's promise of the third of the manor plus £40, had promised to assure £5 per annum from lands in Cambridge (and in fact three years later gave more, £8), on his wife. Kirby had only paid £5 out of the promised £40 'and did practise and go about to defraud and

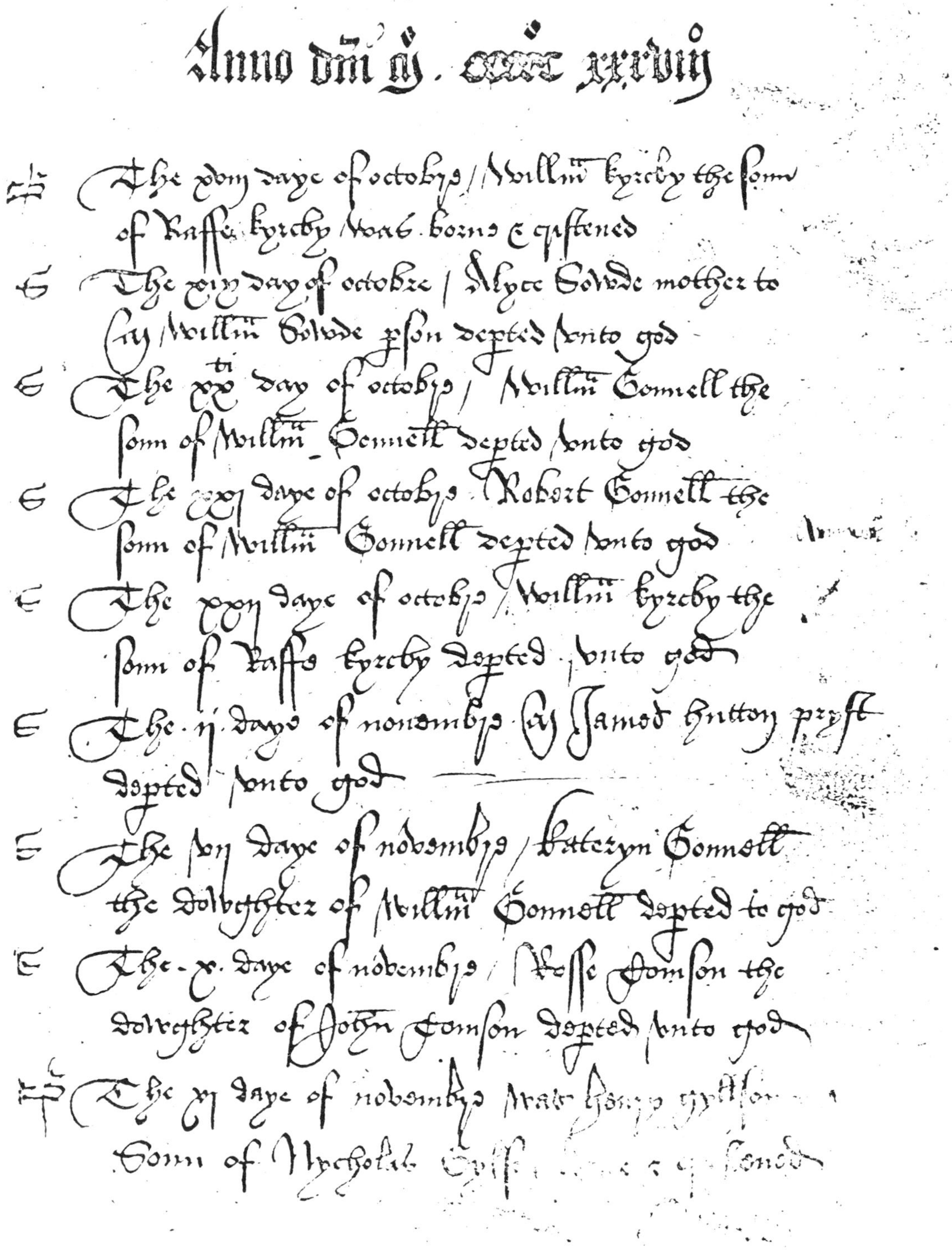

Anno dm' a' . cccc xxxviij

☩ The xviij daye of octobre / Willm' kyrcby the sonn
of Raffe kyrcby Noab. borns e cpstened

☩ The xciij day of octobre / Alyce Golde mother to
Sir Willm' Golde pson depted vnto god

☩ The xx'ti day of octobre / Willm' Gonnell the
sonn of Willm' Gonnell depted vnto god

☩ The xxvj daye of octobre Robert Gonnell the
sonn of Willm' Gonnell depted vnto god

☩ The xxij daye of octobre / Willm' kyrcby the
sonn of Raffe kyrcby depted vnto god

☩ The ij daye of nonembre Sir James Hutton prest
depted vnto god ————

☩ The ix daye of nobembre / Kateryn Gonnell
the dolrghter of Willm' Gonnell depted to god

☩ The x daye of nobembre / Rosse Tomson the
dolrghter of John Tomson depted vnto god

☩ The xj daye of nobembre Water Gryp gryffen
sonn of Nycholdt Gryff . . . . e cpstened

Fig. 9 The first page of the first (paper) parish register during the influenza epidemic of 1538. William, son of Raffe Kirky, was born and christened on the 18th October, 1838, and departed unto God on the 22nd. The villagers interpreted this as an Egyptian Plague. The clerk who wrote a further note called it the 'Sweating Sickness'.

put Hall and his wife and children out of their inheritance of the third part of the manor'. Hall sued him in Chancery. When the case was ready and Kirby knew that he could not win, he talked Hall into dropping his action, promising to deliver his part of the bargain by quarter day (the Nativity of St John the Baptist). But he was only deceiving his son-in-law. Hall had the necessary documents engrossed at his own expense, but Kirby refused to complete the transaction.

Kirby in turn brought an action in Chancery against George Hasell of Huntingdon, Elizabeth's husband. He claimed that George Hasell and others had been entered into bonds 'to make up her jointure in divers other great sums of money' that Kirby could no longer find. He had been taken ill and 'was and yet is impotent, lame and destitute as well of his hearing as of his speech'. He declared that he had given the whole rule and order of his house for love (so he said) to Elizabeth who stayed in Landbeach to look after him. The house in which this part of the drama was acted out must be the timber-framed house of which much of the structure still stands in the interior of Worts farmhouse. Her husband came over from Huntingdon frequently and often stayed on for a week or so. Each time he went home he took a load of the bonds, jewellery or loose cash around the house (which Kirby said amounted to more than £100). All this went to the house at Huntingdon, or to Hasell's confederates, John Richardson and Robert Blinkinghorne.

Then a dreadful thing happened, enough to rend even an honest family

17 Worts Farm from the High Street. The interior still contains much of the structure of the earlier manor house. This range added to the front doubled the size of the house.

apart: Kirby recovered at least enough to realise what his children had done to him! But he could no longer describe with any certainty the appearance or contents of the documents, what sort of containers they were in, 'whether in bag or box, sealed or unsealed, chest locked or otherwise, nor instant value of the goods'.

The legal sparring went on for years. The above account was from the case brought in 1553. In 1559 Hall and Kirby were at each other's throats again, with Kirby trying to reclaim the reversion of the manor. In 1562 there were two arbitrations. Among those appointed as arbitrators was Sir Francis Hinde of Madingley, a much greater sheep-grazier, encloser and abuser of common rights than Kirby himself, almost the perfect stereotype of the period, the 'follower of all things that gain hangeth upon'.

The next major clash between Kirby and his family came when both Hall and Betts sued him in the Common Bench. Thereafter we have little information, but it looks as if Kirby was hell-bent, very much as his sons-in-law claimed, on disinheriting his daughters as well as his sons-in-law. Our last scene in this village drama ends as farce. The marriage register for 1566 has the following note: 'The two and twenty day of October was married Master Richard Kirby and Mistress Margaret Merry-alle: this Master Kirby was carried to church in a chair.' She was a widow. Kirby himself died later the same year. It was his three daughters, and not his sons-in-law, who inherited the manor.

The concentration of school text-book writers on enclosure as the main agrarian problem under the Tudors, has perhaps obscured the very widespread struggling to gain control of the commons in that period, which may have been more fundamental. Even before the Dissolution of the Monasteries flooded the landmarket, gentlemen, or near gentlemen, with wide-ranging interests were to be found moving into our area to pick up whatever came easily to hand.

8

More Gentlemen Ungentle

In 1513 Thomas Thursby of Norfolk was High Sheriff of Cambridgeshire and Huntingdonshire. With his office he brought talents for seizing his opportunities as they came along. In Cottenham, as far back as 1488, he had allowed a house to fall down to separate to himself the common rights belonging to it, especially the profitable grazing of sheep. Cottenham was soon to have the attentions of another large operator. Sir Francis Hinde of Madingley, whom we met as arbitrator for Kirby, had been very active in the fields of Cambridge itself, over-grazing and acquiring small pieces of land without any title to them. In 1560 in Cottenham he was claiming 5,000 acres of fen including two large enclosures for sheepwalk. Thomas Brigham, whom Hinde described as 'a very lewd, perverse and wrangling fellow', along with John Pepys had broken into his enclosures and destroyed his fences. There had been agreements in the 1560s and 1580s giving the lord some right to enclose, but the final agreement came in 1596. This described in detail the enclosures in Longhill, Marehill and Tilling which the lord could keep for himself, yielding up in turn all his common rights. It listed all the tenants with common rights, detailing these. Most important of all in the long-run, it was agreed that no more regulations of the fields should be made by the manor court. The commoners' meetings, with their ordermakers, fen reeves and other officers, took over power. Two of the orderbooks survive, recording variations made from time to time on the Articles, the statutes of a village parliament, one might say. On occasions even the voting for and against any change is recorded.

Some of the lists of ordermakers suggest that the ordermakers were chosen as freeholders and copyholders, manor by manor. Even when this degree of democracy came to the village, the significance of the

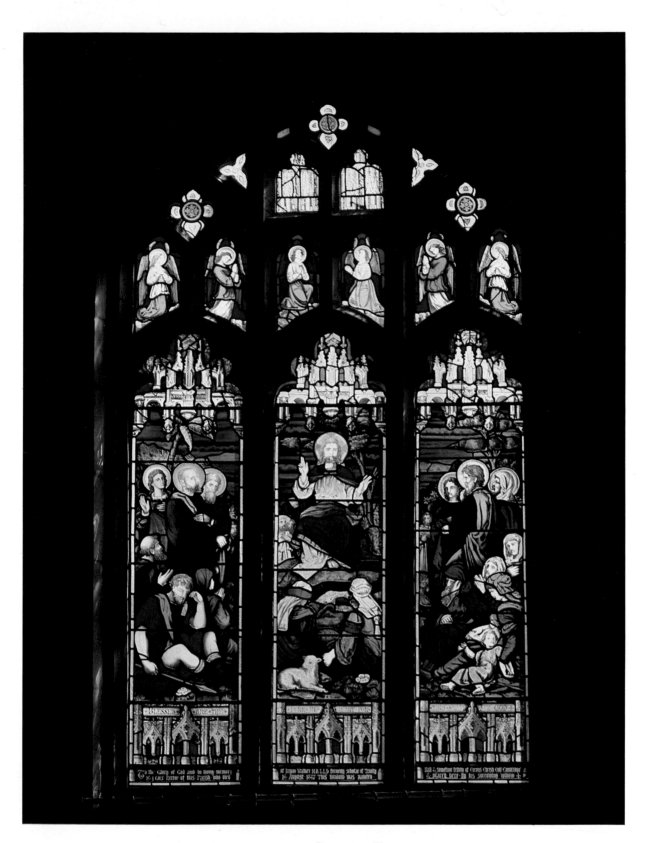

8. The Victorian glass in the east window of the south aisle has some fragments of mediaeval glass in the top lights. *Photo: Richard Muir*

9. (*left*) Detail from the East window: a navigator holding an armillary sphere, used for navigation in the late fourteenth and fifteenth centuries. *Photo: Richard Muir*

10. (*above*) Detail from the East window: a comforting angel. *Photo: Richard Muir*

11. Signs of loving care in the churchyard. Some of the gravestones date back to the seventeenth century. *Photo: Jack Ravensdale*

12. (*right*) On the edge of the village Green which was created in the fifteenth century. The axial chimney suggests that the house was built before the Civil War as an example of the larger type of peasant house, with four rooms on the ground floor and four above. The small square chimney stacks on the gable ends point to later subdivision into a row of four cottages which have subsequently been reunited into two. *Photo: Richard Muir*

13. (*below*) 'The Nest', 34 High Street, very typical of the local cottages of the eighteenth century, now lovingly restored. *Photo: Richard Muir*

14. The late Georgian tradition lingered on in the countryside and gave us that gem of domestic architecture, North Farm. *Photo: Richard Muir*

manors recorded in Domesday was not lost. A small revolution *had* taken place, and Cottenham had acquired a constitution giving extensive powers of self-government. Archdeacon William Cunningham, the pioneer of English Economic History, discerned in this type of arrangement the school of American democracy. Certainly part of the Coolidge family lived in Landbeach and Cottenham.

The Articles of Agreement of 1596 were of the greatest practical value to the peasants and farmers of Cottenham right up to enclosure in 1846, and many copies survive, both printed and in manuscript. It served as the fundamental authority for the detail of social and economic life in Cottenham for two-and-a-half centuries, rather as the Domesday Book did in early mediaeval England.

The rise of the meetings of commoners to a decisive place in the direction and control of the open field agriculture and the management of the fens seems to have come late to Landbeach. An agreement made in 1735 was confirmed by a Decree at Rolls three years later, the College having been cautious in face of the new proposals.

This agreement gave Landbeach something of a written constitution. The fifth article stated:

> That there shall annually be forever a meeting of the Commoners of the said town in the vestry of the Parish Church of Landbeach aforesaid on the first Tuesday in March yearly, at which meeting five proper persons shall be chosen by a majority of the Commoners then present, which five persons shall have power to make orders for the regulation of the common of the said town for that year, which orders shall be binding to all the commons of the said town and the said five persons or the major part of them shall have power to judge and determine what number of bulls are sufficient and shall be kept yearly upon the said common . . .

As so often in family history, we stumble into deep irony as inheritance changes the side on which a family finds itself. John Pepys was one of the leaders of the Cottenham peasantry in their struggle which ultimately led to the 1596 agreement, and was accused by name of riotous behaviour and fence breaking. Hinde's properties in Cottenham passed through marriage to the family of Hobson, the famous Cambridge carrier. His son married Katharine Pepys, taking the property with him, and it went to Katharine in her widowhood. In 1614, the lady of two-and-a-half manors in Cottenham was in dispute with the villagers over the interpretation of the agreement of 1596.

In 1574 a Court of Survey was appointed under, of all people, Sir Francis Hinde, together with Robert Taylor of Landbeach and another.

18 This much repaired but still functional gargoyle, on the fifteenth-century porch of the parish church, must have watched over the first commoners' meetings in the eighteenth century.

This was to settle disputes between the bailiff and the farmer of the manor. It turned out that customs and use were very flexible in spite of the written documents. For example:

The Use of the Commons and Alteration Thereof
Although the customs and uses thereof have and daily do alter according to the disposition of the tenants and officers in the fens, wetness and dryness of the seasons . . . we cannot set down any custom certain, but it may be broken by the discretion of the inhabitants as the times and years shall serve for their best commodity and advantage.

On the east side of Landbeach, Waterbeach had reached its own solution in 1683 by a decree in Chancery, *Articles of agreement for the use of the Commons*. The document lists all the commoners, including those with only half commonable houses, and infants with guardians, who together agree the articles with the lords. They set up a system of regulated stint, making each commoner restricted to his entitlement according to the number of common rights he held. It is very detailed, and the constitution of this powerful new organ of village government is quite clear:

Upon every Thursday next before Christmas Day, between one and four p.m. in the parish church, two fen reeves were to be elected and chosen by the major part of the commoners or their tenants present at the election. They could call for common day works from commoners as they thought necessary to meet any sudden or extraordinary flood. They had to give at least seven days' notice of an annual meeting to fix every commoner's rates to be paid for dyking and fencing. Between this meeting and Lady Day they had to give notice of another meeting in the parish church for making orders and bye laws. At the annual meeting on the Thursday before Christmas Day, the fen reeves were to account to the commoners for their income and expenditure during the year.

We should perhaps observe a little caution as we adopt Cunningham's idea of a school of democracy. In the age of Burke democracy did not have too high a reputation. Robert Masters, the great antiquarian and scholar, was vicar of Waterbeach as well as rector of Landbeach. There is a set of minutes of an eighteenth-century commoners' meeting in Waterbeach. It is in the handwriting of Robert Masters; the chairman is recorded as Robert Masters; and it bears his signature.

The most important common right in Landbeach, the grazing of the sheep flocks, had been divided 'time out of mind', according to the villagers of the mid-seventeenth century. There were four separate sheep-walks: two for Chamberlains, known then as College Sheepwalk and Town Walk (for Chamberlains copyhold tenants); and the Home Walk and Barhill Walk for Brays and their tenants. The numbers allowed were 1,214, 1,220, 1,170 and 1,140 respectively. The parson had a generous allowance in the College Walk.

When Henry Clifford was rector of Landbeach, in the reign of Elizabeth, the lessee of the manor of Chamberlains, a Mr Smith, sued Clifford for the plot of ground opposite the rector's garden, now the children's adventure playground, and won his case, although the plot had been in the rector's hands for over two hundred years.

When the manor of Waterbeach was in the Queen's hand, we find a rather unsavoury group operating there and taking advantage of their offices to line their own pockets. Their dealings took in Landbeach, too. John Yaxley had the lease of Chamberlains manor in 1597, and in 1609 it was taken by Roger Spicer. As well as the arable he had 'all that moor ground or soil called the College Sheepwalk, and the whole liberty of sheepwalk and foldcourse unto the said Master and Fellows (i.e. Corpus Christi College) belonging'.

The year after Spicer took the lease he and his gang of friends appeared in deep trouble at Waterbeach: Sir Miles Sandys, Sir John Peyton, and Sir Simeon Steward were appointed to investigate.

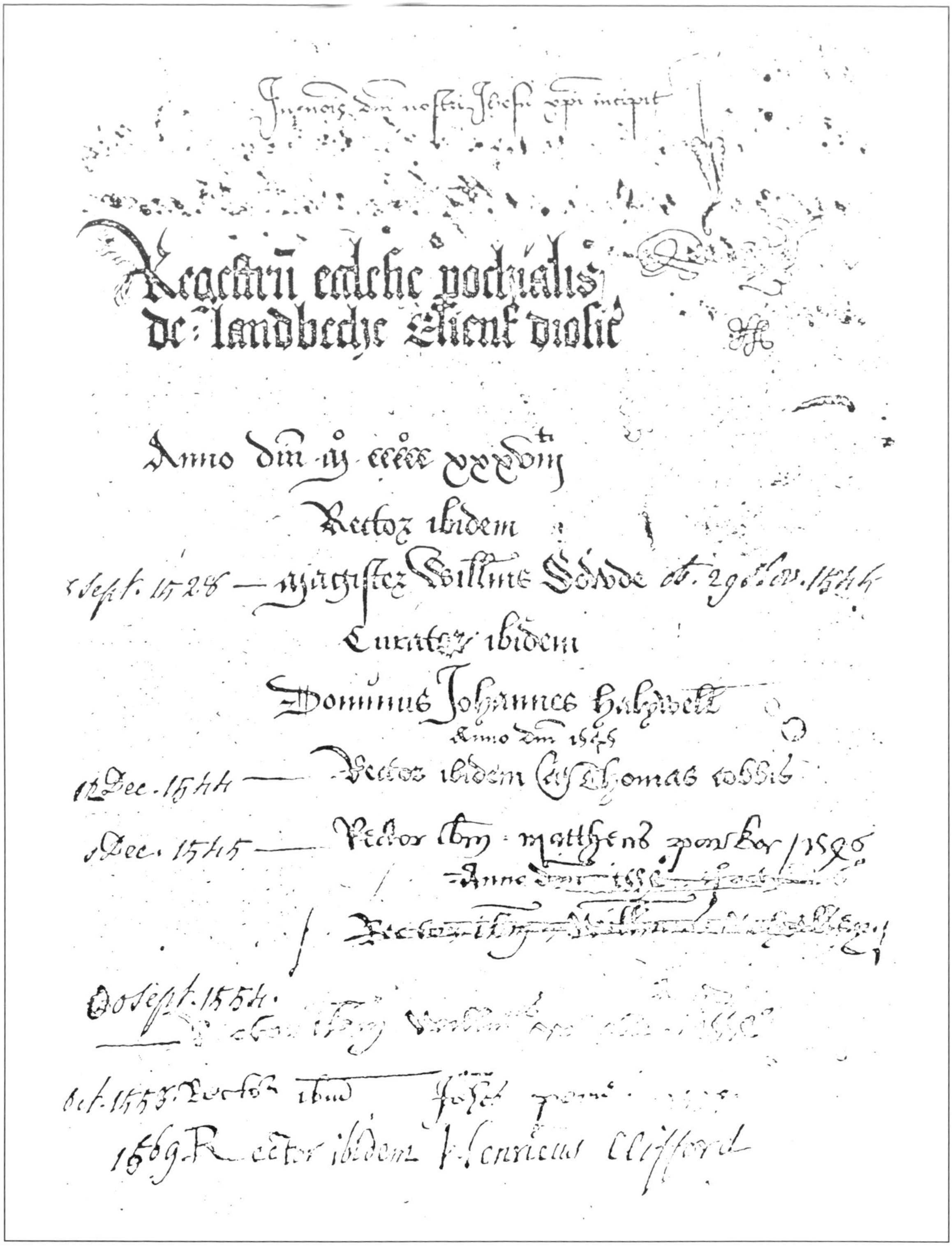

Fig. 10 The title page of the first parish register, with a dedication and the additions of the signatures of later rectors to the end of Elizabeth's reign.

First they examined Roger Woodall, copyholder of the King's Manor of Waterbeach.

He had for three years been under-bailiff, appointed by John Haslop who was supposed to be bailiff, but was a man of straw. Woodall made all his accounts to Spicer, who was son-in-law of John Yaxley, the manorial steward. In the course of the years in which he had held office he had handed over as strays two steers, one heifer, one sow, one mare and one colt, but he did not know if any account had been made to the King's officers.

Yaxley had felled or rooted up timber on an enclosed piece of copyhold land. He had seized the town land to the King's use but had returned it for cash. He retained for his own use £30 which he had taken from the town stock from the churchwardens.

On the way to court on the morning of the examination Yaxley had accosted Woodall and tried to suborn him.

The next man examined, another copyholder of Waterbeach named Mark Charlton, had taken up three copyholdings for which he had paid a fine of £20, their yearly value being £13.6s.8d., as assessed by the Steward, Yaxley and two JPs. Yaxley retained the £20, and when he was in dispute later with the villagers about common rights, he offered Edward Banks £10 back if he would undertake not to join the villagers opposing him. When Banks agreed Yaxley gave him £12, to pass on £2 to Yaxley's son-in-law, Robert Spicer, who kept all the manor courts.

Charlton reported that Yaxley's friend, John Haslop of Trumpington, held the title of bailiff, but that Yaxley and his son-in-law, Spicer, jointly executed the office, and had done so since Haslop took the name. He went into some detail about Yaxley's dealings in timber, illegal felling, pulling up, and taking away to the village or Cambridge itself. He confirmed with more detail the account of Yaxley's getting his hands on the town stock from the churchwardens, and the £10 refund of Edward Banks's fine.

Fortunately their learning does not seem to have been exclusively the Parable of the Unjust Steward. The Robson Charity and the alms houses in Waterbeach were really founded by Yaxley, and passed to Robsons, the name under which the Charity is now known, by way of the Spicers. It would seem that ill-gotten gains may be well spent, and there may be occasions when the good that men do may not be interred with their bones.

*   *   *

19 Glebe House, an example of the relatively rare type of pre-Civil War house with four rooms up and four down. Norfolk reed makes a very fine thatch.

The hundred years between the Dissolution of the Monasteries and the Civil War saw almost unlimited possibilities for speculation in land. The Pepys family were to be found at one time and another active in all our villages around Landbeach, sometimes on a small scale, at others more substantially. Office-holding could also be turned to good account in boosting the family fortunes. From the thirteenth century they had been the most prominent family in the Cottenham manor held by Crowland Abbey, where they were regular holders of such key local offices as were performed by villeins. After the Black Death they were almost constantly involved in the land market, and did well enough to practise money-lending in their native village.

William Pepys was bailiff of the Cottenham manor when Crowland Abbey was dissolved. Most conveniently, when it became necessary, he could produce a lease which was dated back far enough for it to be accepted as legal, when too many leases were such obvious fabrications that it was clear they were clumsy attempts to take advantage of the times. The Pepys took their opportunities also, but took them efficiently. How many families emerged from villeinage as it faded in the late fifteenth century, to be represented in the House of Lords in three generations?

To achieve the very best results in the land market it was necessary to use care in the marriage market as well, where it was all too easy to get lost in trackless wastes. In 1558 we find John Pepys complaining to the Lord Chancellor. He said that he 'was moved and procured by one Alice Harrison (the wife of Thomas Harrison, gent.) to become a suitor in marriage unto Edith Talbot, the daughter of the said Alice (Talbot, now Harrison)'. He took the bait and 'travailled in the said suit'.

Alice, like an angler seeing the float bob, struck. She 'perceived him to be in some towardness of matrimony with the said Edith' and, having three unmarried daughters 'whose portion to advance them in matrimony was very small', she begged Pepys 'in consideration of her good-will' that as a condition of marriage, he would agree to surrender to her a legacy of £40 left to Edith by her father. It was still unpaid in the hands of Alice and her current husband, Thomas Harrison. Should he marry Edith, John Pepys was to give the legacy to Alice Harrison. But then the latter, advised by the son of a former marriage, Richard Skott, refused the offer of the legacy and asked Pepys for £40 from his own property instead, and in addition a life interest in some copyhold lands in Cotten-ham. All this had to be kept secret from Thomas Harrison. Pepys thought that this was asking a little too much and refused.

Alice and Skott played their counter-stroke: they bore Edith off to Northamptonshire, far from John Pepys, 'and there kept her close and hidden from him, whereby he was more troubled and driven to spend more money and a large time in seeking where to find, and how he might come to speak with the said Edith.' Under the strain he broke and agreed to be bound both to pay the £40 to Alice, and to give the assurance of the copyhold lands.

Unfortunately again, as so often with this class of record, the outside of the roll is worn and abraded illegibly, and we do not have the result of the case. Other sources, however, tell us that they were in the end married, that Edith lived until 1583, and that John, after a second marriage, lasted until 1589. It is from the union of John and Edith that one of the more important branches of the family were descended: Talbot Pepys was the Recorder of Cambridge under the Commonwealth. Land-beach was well into the zone of operation of the family: in 1549 Roger Pepys lived where Old Beach Farm now stands. In 1630 and again in 1650 we find Richard Pepys as steward of the manor of Brays.

The parsons of Waterbeach and Milton were very frequently among those presented at the mediaeval courts for trespassing and grazing with large flocks where they had no right. They could also be mixed up in more sordid deals. A vicar of Waterbeach was involved in one such.

Robert Cooper died, leaving behind a mentally handicapped wife, and a son in a similar state. His wife, Joan, was possessed of a copyhold in Waterbeach. In view of Joan's state it was easy to persuade her to marry David Manning, 'a man of no worth'. Manning sold the copyhold, a messuage and four-and-a-half acres of land, to the vicar, who seems to have taken responsibility for the boy's maintenance, taking for this five times the sixpence a year which he paid to Thomas Corte, to whom he sub-contracted the care of the boy.

The case was raised in the Court of Requests, otherwise known as the Court of Poor Men's Pleas. When it came to trial, the whole issue turned on the capability of the Coopers, mother and son, to be responsible in law. Robert Austin of Waterbeach declared that he had known them for upwards of ten years, and as to the son: 'He thinketh him to be a simple man of small understanding because he knoweth not how to govern himself as well as other men commonly do.' Joan, the mother, 'was accounted among the neighbours for a woman of simple will, but he doth not well know what is meant by the word idiot.' Here, for once, the true authentic voice of the peasant comes through to us.

9

All Saints

In common with almost all other Cambridgeshire villages, Landbeach has no mention of its church in the Domesday Book. Such absences can have no significance because there clearly were churches in some places that do not mention them in the entry.

In about 1098, Picot the sheriff, in fulfilment of a vow made by his wife when she was sick near to death, founded a house of Augustinian canons at St Giles on Castle Hill in Cambridge. His nephew, Payne de Peverel, moved the house to Barnwell in 1119 or thereabouts, and he also made over to the canons tithes from Landbeach parish church. Anglo-Saxon minsters (colleges of priests who lived a common life but served the churches of a wide area of several parishes) were frequently converted into Augustinian houses by the Normans, and it seems likely that Picot's foundation was one of them. The fact that Landbeach tithes were paid to the canons appears to indicate that the parish may have been served by their predecessors.

Old people in Landbeach, when the oldest church there of which we have any knowledge was being built, may have remembered the Domesday Commission. A couple of years ago this statement could not have been made: it was only during the very recent restoration of the East end that some good Norman stonework that had been re-used was discovered. Previously we had thought the first stone in the present church to date from the thirteenth century. A finely cut piece of chevron decoration and a scalloped capital mean that we must look for a stone church in Landbeach a century or more further back than we did before.

All the earlier work in the church is of Northamptonshire limestone. When the quarries from which this had come began to run out, the much softer and less satisfactory Cambridgeshire clunch, which is merely lower,

20 Good, dressed limestone in the foundations of Old Beach Farmhouse could have come from the ruined Chamberlains manor house across the way.

and slightly harder, beds of chalk, began to be used. This has resulted in early work, like the tracery in the main East window, surviving almost as strong as ever, while the much later clerestory windows are very badly crumbled.

In common with most fen-edge parishes, Landbeach has the remains of a mediaeval canal system which includes a dock that would have had deeper water than most of the small commercial hithes. This larger dock would have taken the barge that carried the stone to build the church and possibly the manor house. The lower courses around the south-west corner and the north end of Old Beach Farm use blocks of dressed limestone, and many clunch blocks are used in nearby garden walls. Some of the limestone is pink as if calcined by fire. The site of the old manor house of the Chamberlains is quite near, across the road, and the probability is that the good stone at the north end of the village was robbed from what may long have been a ruin, having succumbed to fire and flood even before it was purchased by the College.

The few Norman fragments do not enable us to reconstruct the plan of the church at that date, but there are some hints as to the plan of its Early English successor. The examination of the roof during the restoration of 1868–78 showed that the rafters had been reduced in length when the pitch of the roof was changed. The plaster on the tower's east side, seen from inside the nave, shows that the Early English church had a lower ridge but a steeper pitched roof. At that time it would have had a continuous roof over both nave and narrow aisle at the same pitch. The chancel of this thirteenth-century church (we might probably call it the Chamberlains' church since that family must almost certainly have built it) was a simple aisleless hall, very similar to what we see today, and indeed most of it is still there, disguised by later insertions. A fourteenth-century Decorated window has been inserted in the south wall of the chancel within a hidden arch of the earlier period, now invisible under plaster. But the two priest's doors, north and south, are both from the Early English church, belonging to a building phase that probably came to a climax with the great East window, and the small, double piscina in the south aisle.

Belonging to this period also, now gone without trace, is a Chamberlain mortuary chapel beyond the east end of the south aisle. This must have been very small as the aisle was narrower, and the priest's door in the south wall of the chancel seems to have been then where it still is now, thus restricting the length east and west of the chapel. The tower belonged to this early church, too, but would then have been without the buttresses and spire.

Near the top of the tower, on the north side, is a badge of Corpus Christi on its own, not combined with the badge of the Blessed Virgin Mary. After 1359, when the College began to acquire the manor and patronage, the badges of both Guilds would have been combined.

The passing of the Early English features in one or more major rebuildings can be watched in the report of the architect in 1868:

All the curves and framing above the tie-beams, and the tie-beams themselves, may have been and probably were in an Early English roof to the nave, as they are much larger than they would be if constructed *de novo* at the date of their erection in their present form.

I think there was at the time the clerestory was added, a good substantial oak roof, and that the beams were moulded on their lower edges before they were re-fixed. The principal rafters have been plainly cut short at the purlins, with a view to keeping down the height of the roof as was needful of course, if an Early English roof was to be converted to a Perpendicular one. The mouldings of the beams above the purlins are uniformly different from those below.

About 1450, Nicholas Toftys of Landbeach constructed a new roof of St Benet's Church, then used by the College of Corpus Christi as their chapel. The present roof of All Saints, Landbeach, is contemporary, and so probably the work of Nicholas Toftys also. It is probably to his hand that we owe the lovely carved angels, in feathered suits like actors in Mystery plays, and the patrons with shields who adorn the hammers between each pair of tie-beams. These could be visited and inspected at close quarters for the first time during the restoration of the roof. It was then that Dr Richard Muir pointed out that the last tie-beam against the tower, and the wall-plate of the south aisle, had green men, with vine-leaves sprouting from their mouths. So this pagan symbol was quietly inserted, where it would not attract attention, but where those who knew could see it, in a Christian church in the fifteenth century. A hundred years before, such creatures, almost hidden by their own foliage, made their way into the Lady Chapel at Ely.

There would seem to have been three major reconstructions of the Old English Church. In the fourteenth century windows were inserted in the Decorated style, in the south side of the chancel, and in the tower, and the latter was strengthened by the addition of the new style diagonal French buttresses. The clerestory was probably added in the early fifteenth century on to a reconstructed nave, when the mansard roof introduced yet a third pitch over the nave.

By this time the interior had been adapted for quite elaborate ritual. What has for a long time been called the Chamberlain Monument in the north wall is a fine example of a common type of Easter Sepulchre. Here the Host, consecrated at the last Mass before Good Friday, would be ceremonially entombed, watched over by two women representing Mary and Martha. At the first Mass on Easter morning another procession would be led by the priests to the sepulchre where the Gospel would be sung as dialogue, beginning, 'Whom Seekest Thou?', in Latin, '*Quem quaeritis?*' Then another procession, which tended to become more and more elaborate, would take the Host back to the High Altar. In this way drama and the liturgy went together.

21 (*above*) The splendid fifteenth-century church roof has alternate tie-beams and hammer beams, with benefactors and angels in feathered suits.

22 (*right*) One of the fine carved figures on the hammer-beam ends. All have lost their wings.

23 (*far right*) The north aisle has a set of particularly striking smaller figures. We hope that the ravages of the beetle have been stayed.

24 A 'green man', a pagan symbol, with leaves growing from his mouth, in the fifteenth-century woodwork of the parish church. One of three.

John and Thomas Lane, by wills dated 1519, as had William Richard in 1504, left money to endow the light kept at the Sepulchre during the vigil. Edmund Lane followed their example in 1530. Then the Reformation came, the ceremony disappeared, the tradition was lost, and folk forgot what this strange blind, low arch in the thickness of the wall had been. It is largely through wills that we get glimpses of the elaboration of the ritual, and of the social life of the village church in the later Middle Ages. By this time the rood screen and loft had come to divide the priest's part of the church, the chancel and sanctuary, from the nave where, in the early days, the congregation in the murk assisted at the service in the French sense of the word; they stood and watched the drama of the Mass in the East end, lit up by the great East windows.

During the great restoration of 1868–78, the rector of the time, Bryan Walker, with the help of the architects, carried out something of an archaeological investigation of the chancel screen. They concluded that there had once been two screens, and challenged the tradition that Masters had brought the tower screen to the chancel arch when he had pulled down the Lady Chapel at the north-east corner to make the church symmetrical. Some of the woodwork carved in the fourteenth century he used in his charity cottages, and part went elsewhere on the Green. The

Fig. 11 The Easter Sepulchre in the north wall of the church, incorrectly known for centuries as the Chamberlain Monument. From 'Notes upon Discoveries made during the recent restoration of Landbeach Church, by the Rev Bryan Walker, MA, LID, Rector' in Cambridge Antiquarian Communications, No.XXI, 1881, p. 250, *with thanks to the Cambridge Antiquarian Society.*

lower part of the existing screen, the *dado*, certainly appears to be in its rightful place, and the upper part of the tracery is of the same period. The middle section matches for period, late Decorated style, but the pieces will not fit into any fourteenth-century pattern. Their placing is undoubtedly not original. It is easy, too, to see that the fleurons on the beam have been moved to keep equal intervals while spanning a wider space.

Bryan Walker also decided that the pulpit was original mediaeval, and had been part of an original composition in which were joined benches, screen and pulpit. The tracery on the pulpit he thought was additional embellishment from the collection of mediaeval woodwork that Masters had brought to the church when Jesus College threw it out. The tracery probably does belong to that source, but the panels are probably mediaeval only in style.

Wherever there was a piscina (a wash-basin for the holy vessels in the thickness of the wall), there would have been an altar. Thus, just to the left of the priest's door into the vestry, the old wall, which survives from the old Lady Chapel, has a piscina; there is also a square, double piscina in the south chancel wall to serve the main High Altar. The Gothic double piscina in the south wall of the nave, near the East end, indicates a side chapel, and Bryan Walker guessed that this was the chapel of St James. It was so re-dedicated in 1973 in memory of a recent rector. The problem is that the piscina in the south aisle ante-dates the plan of the Lady Chapel that Masters pulled down.

There were at least two village guilds. The All Hallows Guild seems to have been principal since the dedication of the church is to All Saints, and the Guildhall was built as a house for the All Hallows Guild. The Jesus Guild seems to have had a picture of Christ with a light before it, as there was in front of the other images, the Virgin Mary, Our Lady of Pity, Our Lady (at the chancel door), Our Lady again in the Lady Chapel, and one of St Nicholas. Bryan Walker's imaginative reconstruction of the plan of the church as it might have been about 1450 shows the west bays of the aisles screened off as guild chapels, and he himself claimed to have removed the screens during the restoration.

The insertion of more and larger windows in the nave, the raising of the aisle roof to allow still taller windows, and the relative cheapness of glass which made more window space acceptable, brought full light to the nave for the first time, and the development of guild and side chapels brought more of the action of the liturgy down into the nave where the people were, and by such means as processions, and voluntary work looking after the images, altars and chapels, involved the laity more in the life and worship of the church.

15. (*above*) Timber-framed construction carefully restored to make a marvellous setting for a homely environment. *Photo: Richard Muir*

16. (*right*) Copt Hall has some exceptionally fine late mediaeval timbering and window frames. It has been preserved and restored by the Cottage Improvement Society. *Photo: Richard Muir*

17. The author's house, 21 High Street, undergoing rethatching. A tremendous quantity of materials seems to be required. *Photo: Jack Ravensdale*

18. 'Clay Bat' construction used in an outbuilding. With a brick skin, it was used to build many of the village houses. *Photo: Jack Ravensdale*

19. The Plague House before restoration, from the south. The building is part mediaeval. This wing was originally of one floor only, open to the roof. The end dormer was inserted early this century to make an additional bedroom. *Photo: Jack Ravensdale*

20. Restoration work proceeding on the Plague House. At one time the village Post Office, the wooden structure on the corner of the house in this picture was the first telephone kiosk in the village. The house, fully restored, can be seen in the photograph on p. 136. *Photo: Jack Ravensdale*

21. Old Beach Farm, a splendid house at the change from old to new fashions in its time. The early pink brick is particularly attractive. It appears in a seventeenth-century list as 'John Annis's brick house'. *Photo: Richard Muir*

22. Number 34 High Street before restoration. *Photo: Jack Ravensdale*

23. Trinity Hall Cottage: another eighteenth-century cottage before restoration. *Photo: Jack Ravensdale*

24. Glebe House before restoration. Several thatched cottages in the village had corrugated iron to cover the roof when thatchers were in short supply. As thatchers became available again, so restoration took place. The restored house appears in the photograph on p. 86. *Photo: Jack Ravensdale*

25 The pulpit appears to be made up from genuine mediaeval wooden tracery on more modern panels.

26 The double piscina at the east end of the south aisle means that there was another side chapel here in the late thirteenth century.

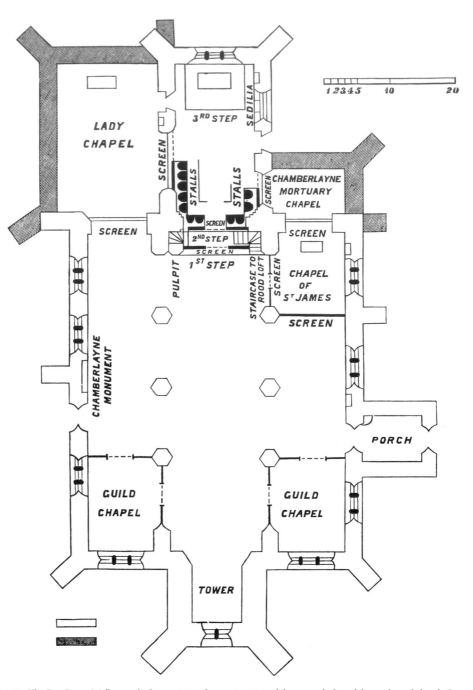

Fig. 12 The Rev Bryan Walker made this conjectural reconstruction of the ground-plan of the mediaeval church. From 'Notes upon Discoveries made during the recent restoration of Landbeach Church, by the Rev Bryan Walker, MA, LID, Rector' in Cambridge Antiquarian Communications, No.XXI, 1881, p. 247, *with thanks to the Cambridge Antiquarian Society.*

In addition the church had acquired more colour, more than it has today, from stained-glass windows and painted walls. The glorious mixture of coloured fragments of mediaeval glass in the windows of All Saints, Landbeach, in the heads of the windows in the south aisle, seem to be almost entirely pieces that fit. Images in them were defaced, but enough remained for the knowledgeable expert to be able to fit these top lights together again. The rest of the mediaeval glass once in these windows has gone. The great East window is very different. These fragments have been fitted together into a frame that was never meant to take them. The quality of most of the glass, as well as the quantity, is very rare for a small parish church. Some of the fragments, especially those of very intense colour, are exceptionally old. The heads seem to be of the fifteenth century, and the one at the top, with his armillary sphere, could well be one of the sea-travellers going to new worlds. The lovely Madonna-like head in the centre is thought to be Lady Margaret Beaufort, with her parents, the grand-parents of Henry VII, on either side.

27 The central figure of the East window is said to be the Lady Margaret Beaufort. The glass, said to come from Wimborne Minster in Dorset, was brought to Landbeach by Robert Masters.

28 A corbel head in the form of a musician still helps support the roof after five centuries.

Rows of angels in the stained-glass lights in the south aisle have lost their heads, as have those on the corbel stones in the Chapel of Saint James. Such breaking of 'superstitious images' was common in this area during both the Reformation and the Civil War. What is remarkable at Landbeach is that, apart from the glass, so much survives intact. Such vandalism does not seem to have been taken up by the parishioners with any more haste than was absolutely forced upon them. In the parish register, among the entries for the year 1562, a person who was literate but lacking in orthography has written (presumably without authority), 'Pope the fox will eat no grapes and why, he cannot get them, so at this town they love English service because they can have none other, as appeareth by the candle-beam and rood loft as I think. Judge you by me, Nicholas Nemo AD 1594.'

About thirty years ago a rector began to find fragments of stained glass in the garden, some of it very old indeed. For a while he thought he was about to discover the whole of the mediaeval glass of the church. Alas, it soon petered out. There had once been a stained-glass window in the rectory, which, among other things, bore the legend *Adam da Deo Gloriam*, and it is possible that this dated from the long incumbency of Master Adam Clerke in the fifteenth century. The glass in the East window was placed there by Robert Masters, and it is now thought that he got it from Wimborne Minster in Dorset.

Masters brought back even more colour to the interior. In 1787 he gave a picture of the Adoration of the Shepherds by the Flemish master Joachim Beuckelaer, dated 1563. It was a fine picture and Masters installed it as a reredos. The great restoration of 1878 raised the East end progressively up a series of steps with the unfortunate result that the picture was part hidden by the altar and stuck up at the top in front of the lower part of the window. It was housed temporarily in the grand entrance hall of the rectory which had been created by Masters. There it remained temporarily until the church authorities decided to sell the rectory. The conditions of temperature and humidity in the church were unfit for the picture. It was sold and the proceeds used to restore the north aisle.

The Adoration was the work of a master, but it was unsuccessful as a reredos. Mediaeval churches, and that of Landbeach not least, had other ways of cheering and teaching the people through colour: wall paintings. Only tiny fragments of these now remain in Landbeach: some red colouring on the arch from the north aisle into the old Lady Chapel; and some fragments of vine scroll with tiny bunches of grapes in wine colour behind the pulpit. Probably this was preserved by the old arrangement of the pulpit with its sounding-board covering the design. It is from the fourteenth century.

Much wall-painting in the church survived until 1857 when flaking was followed by the decision to chip back to the stone and re-plaster. Some amateur sketches of the better preserved pictures were made before the destruction. The most striking of all seems to have been a well-built blonde angel in a diaphanous loose gown, above the chancel arch. Another angel, with outspread wings, was holding a cross. There was a man holding a tree in his hand, presumably Jesse. A man portrayed against a background of buildings looks very much like St Christopher as depicted in some other nearby churches. It is galling to think that the whole of the church must have been generously endowed with colour and painted stone, and that most of it survived into the second half of the nineteenth century, only to be gone now.

Much mediaeval woodwork is built into the pews west of the cross passage between the two nave doors. One pew, which we think of as the blacksmith's seat, has a farrier's tools—horse-shoe, nails, pincers and hammer—included in the decoration on the panels. This may have had

Fig. 13 Sketches made of the crumbling wall-paintings in the church in 1857, before they were destroyed.

a special significance for the villagers, but is hardly rustic in quality. Exact, fine and neat, it would have been quite acceptable to Jesus College, from which it may have come.

The Victorian Communion table was newly constructed, but bears small panels of mediaeval work inserted for decoration. Two Laudian Communion tables are now degraded to office table in the parson's vestry, and to carrying books and pamphlets by the door. The finest piece of woodwork that the church had was the north door which went to Ely Cathedral in 1821. The then vicar of Waterbeach persuaded the rector of Landbeach to transfer it to Ely without consulting the parish. The vicar was already a prebend of Ely: I hope he had a further preferment!

There is a history to the Royal arms no longer in the church. During the Commonwealth the wardens paid Goodman Lawrence for defacing the King's Arms two shillings. At the Restoration they paid to the painters for setting up the King's Arms two pounds and five shillings. In 1826 the

29 Some of the symbols of the farrier's craft in one of the mediaeval pews in the church.

carved wooden arms, which Dr Gunning had placed in the College Hall at Corpus Christi, were given to Landbeach church, and the old arms, which in 1745 had been reported as hanging over the chancel screen, were passed on to Milton Church. In much more recent times Corpus Christi, lords of the manor and patrons of the living of All Souls, Landbeach, took the old arms back in exchange for help with church bells restoration, and beautified them for their hall again.

The piece of woodwork that attracts most attention from visitors is the lectern, a wooden angel, almost life-sized, with upraised hands and wings supporting the book. It is reported to have been purchased in York (or possibly New York) and to be of Dutch origin.

But of all the woodwork in the church, the oldest piece is the very heavy iron-bound parish chest which has been attributed by experts to the thirteenth or fourteenth century.

Early in Robert Masters' incumbency, he decided to re-arrange some of the pews, and to make a secure fit the workmen struck off a stone rose projecting from the north-east pillar about four feet above ground level. In a cavity behind the rose were:

> Two wooden dishes, nicely carved and cemented together, with some linen cloth, the remains of which were still visible and in them, as the skilful in anatomy fully assert, the muscular part of a human heart which, after being properly prepared by the embalmers as was evident from some parts remaining of their preparations, had likewise been carefully wrapped up in linen, the threads whereof were yet distinctly visible; the dishes had been afterwards filled up with what had indeed the appearance of either hair or wool, but, upon a nicer examination being found to have many fibres, must rather have been some vegetable substance; and perhaps, making some allowance for the alterations made therein through length of time, might have been spikenard, much used on such occasions.

It was shown to both the Royal and Antiquarian Societies, and was deposited in the British Museum, much to the anger of William Cole who for a time was Masters' curate as well as antiquarian rival. It subsequently disappeared.

* * *

To what is still visible we can add what the words of so many bequests tell us of the spiritual life of the later Middle Ages. In Landbeach, however, these begin as far back as a few years before the Black Death, with Henry Chamberlain who wished his whole estate to go for masses for his soul and for distribution to the poor of the parish.

30 Unique to Landbeach, the angel-lectern was purchased in York and is thought to be of Dutch workmanship.

The next surviving will is from over a century later, in 1479. It is from the lord of the manor of Brays, William Keteriche, who starts off, as so many wills do, with money to the parson for 'tithes forgotten'. Bequests to religious houses were still quite popular, and the family had connections with Denney Abbey, just across the parish border in Waterbeach. He left the abbess and convent there 66s.8d. to keep his anniversary, and those of his benefactors, and his parents. There is provision for his daughter on her marriage, and for the care of her up to full age. Should she die first, the whole of the bequest to Denney should be diverted to keeping her anniversary in perpetuity. Ten pounds more was left to the abbey for his daughter's taking vows there. He left a further forty shillings to the Abbess of Denney and to Dame Agnes Keteriche, his sister, and Dame Elizabeth, his daughter, and he repaid a debt of ten pounds from his father to the abbey.

By the time of Henry Lane's will in 1493, family bequests are taking a more prominent place, but he left twenty shillings to Denney Abbey to pray for him, and two shillings for the abbess' rabbits that he had poached. He seems to have had family connections in Waterbeach, too, since he left two shillings to the high altar, and twenty shillings for mending the roads there. The switch away from monasteries to parish churches and masses there had begun as a general pattern in bequests, but the others did not stop at once. He appointed a chantry priest to sing and pray for a year for him. All the children of the family and all the godchildren were to have a ewe and a lamb each. To his son Henry he left his creke plough and four mares, and his little macer with two silver spoons, and to Thomas his old macer with two silver spoons. In the last generation before the Reformation the better-off families of laity seem extra-extravagant in their pious bequests. Six shillings and eightpence for funeral torches seems almost to become a hallmark of respectability.

The chaplain, Dominus John Sweyn, in 1496 left 6s.8d. for torches and another 6s.8d. to keep a taper for him burning in the church in front of Our Lady of Pity, to have pity on his soul as long as the fund lasted. It was a generous will even for a man with no dependants: 20s. to repair the bells, 10s. to Denney Abbey, 12d. to every household in Landbeach, a book called *Pupilla Oculi* to Master Cosyn (the Master of Corpus Christi), and his little portforium (a form of attaché case) to Master Saintwary (a fellow of the College and future rector of Landbeach).

There seems to be a change of atmosphere in the generation before the breach with Rome. In 1519 John Lane bequeathed 20s. for paving of the streets, a legacy becoming very common in the period; 11s. to the All Hallows Guild for building a guildhall for it; and small bequests to nearby village churches. Nothing is here for any religious house. Their popularity seems to have been in temporary decline. Thomas Lane's will, made later the same year, is concerned with the high altar, church repair, the bells, the sepulchre light, the guild, 12d. to every householder, the four orders of friars in Cambridge, and again to nearby parish churches. There is a gradual shift in the direction of pious bequests from prayers and masses for the benefactors' souls, and lights before the images and the rood, to family bequests. By 1521 Robert Kirby leaves the manor place of Brays to his wife.

Some wills become very earthy. Robert Gray, styled gentleman, left twenty ewes, each with a lamb, and a cow with calf to each of his three daughters, and three hundred loads of gravel to the town. Gravel for the roads seems badly needed at this time to judge from the number of bequests. My predecessor by four centuries in the house where I live, in Queen Mary's reign left 5s. to the parson, 40s. to the church, 6s.8d. to the poor box, and 5s. to the highways, as well as a host of bequests to

31 A gargoyle near the top of the tower.

family and benefactors. The bequest to the parson was the common one, 'for tithes forgotten'. In this reign many followed his wise course and used the standard simplest form of salutation at the head of the will, 'In the name of God Amen. First, I bequeath my soul to Almighty God etc.' This is in the early days of Philip and Mary, and tight-rope walking would be the order of the day. Thirty-three years later there is another will of another Nicholas Aunger, 'In *primis*, I give and betake my soul into the hands of Almighty God, trusting to be saved through Jesus Christ.'

The whole of this will gives a picture of a sixteenth-century village family and household:

Item, I give and bequeath unto Richard Aunger and Henry Aunger, my sons, and unto Marie and Elizabeth, my daughters, the crop of thirteen acres of corn, the profits thereof, being equally divided amongst them, and the rent of the land due at the Feast of St Michael the Archangel next and immediately ensuing being likewise of them equally borne and paid.

Item, the lease that I have of the said land and others thereunto appertaining after the feast of St Michael the Archangel next coming, I give unto William Colle so as he marry my daughter Elizabeth, they, yielding and paying unto Richard, Henry and Marie, my children beforenamed, yearly 20s. to be equally divided amongst them, during the time and term of the said lease.

Item, I give and bequeath unto Henry my son my great brass pan, a brass pot and another smaller pot, and four pieces of pewter (viz. two platters and two dishes) and my cloak, and three candlesticks, my great chest and three sheets and one table napkin being therein. Also my old cupboard and my two ballchynes.

Item, I give and bequeath to Richard my son two brass pans and my best heifer and my long cart body and a dung cart with the wheels.

Item, I give and bequeath unto Marie, my daughter, my biggest brass pot and a posnet, a kettle, three platters, one pewter dish, one saucer, two porringers, a saltcellar, two candlesticks, a cupboard, a cupboard cloth, two pairs of sheets, a bearing sheet, two pillow beers, one pillow, a yard kercher, a mattress, two blankets, and my red cow with the white face, and my young red pied cow, two table napkins, a table cloth, a feather bolster, a joined bedstead with a painted tester, and curtain drawers.

Item, my two colts I give equally to be divided among my four children before named.

The residue of all my goods and chattels unbequeathed I give unto

Elizabeth my daughter and unto William Colle, if he shall marry my said daughter, whom I ordain and make my executors.

Item, I desire Master Henry Clifford to be my supervisor unto my will, and to advertise (advise) and counsel my children.

These being witness, John Aunger, Henry Gotobed, Richard Badricke, and Richard Moor of Landbeach.

Memorandum, that the 8th day of May, 1589, the forenamed William Colle and Elizabeth Aunger were lawfully joined together in matrimony in the parish church of Landbeach aforesaid and so I witness by the signing of these presents with my hand and name the day and year above written

By me Henry Clifford, Clerk.

32 An eighteenth-century headstone near the church porch.

The will was written on 16th April the same year. Not much grass had grown. The will, in all probability, represents or includes part of a marriage settlement.

The change to the 'matter-of-fact', which can be seen in the surviving wills of the seventeenth century, shows something of the bareness in the church where the torches and lights have all gone, and the images, windows and wall paintings are all defaced. William Hadsley made a particularly pious will for a man of Landbeach a few months before the death of Mary Tudor: '. . . whole in mind and of good remembrance, thanks be given to Almighty God . . . first I bequeath my soul to the merciful hands of God my Maker and Redeemer Jesus Christ, to Our Blessed Lady St Mary, and to all the Company of Heaven, and my body to be buried in the churchyard . . .'

This was in some contrast to Matthew Parker's curate, Henry Johnson. He gave the minimum attention to religious formulae: 'I bequeath my soul to Almighty God, and my body to be buried in the parish church-yard . . .'

Some of the changes in bequests to religious houses were inevitable. Once it was suspected that the government had its eyes on the property of the religious houses, guilds and chantries, no testator could expect bequests to such to be anything but wasted. Perhaps the curate was one of the wisest men in the village, realising that safety, at that time, lay more in avoiding offence rather than in the attempt to win approval. After all, his old master, Matthew Parker, was none too safe in Norfolk.

Whether the phrases represent the views of testator or scribe, they seem to suggest that the laity were more ready to follow fashion, one beat behind the band, where the clergy had learned discretion. But it is difficult to compare the almost intangible spiritual life of a parish some centuries ago with that of the same church today. In 1728 the Landbeach parson, Micklebourgh, was resident in Benet College (Corpus Christi). He celebrated Holy Communion six times a year with an average of a dozen communicants. By comparison, in this age of apostasy we have grounds for hope.

10

At Home

The better wills give some idea of family life and family management; of the place of the affections and the business of matrimonial alliance. They also give a few hints, as we saw, of religious belief in the village community. There is another prolific source which sheds light on the homes and lives of the villagers, probate inventories. Often, in listing the goods and chattels of a person, room by room through the house, these virtually give a verbal snapshot of the house as it was when the householder died.

Among the Landbeach families who left such accounts of their household arrangements were the Taylors, who rose steadily to be one of the most substantial village families by the time of the Parliamentary Enclosure in 1813. The principal house where they lived and to which the inventory of Robert in 1691 seems to refer is Old Beach Farm, probably the first brick house in the village.

A true and perfect inventory of the goods and chattels of Robert Taylor, late of Landbeach in the county of Cambridge deceased, taken and apprised upon the 6th day of May, Anno Dni 1691 by us whose names are hereunto subscribed.

	£ s d
Inprimis his apparel and money in his purse	30:00:00

In the Hall

It. 2 tables 12 joined stools, one fire grate, a fire shovel a pair of tongs a birding piece and a traverse valued at	02:19:00

In the Kitchen

It. 8 pewter dishes 4 brass pots 4 kettles 2 skillets a pestle and mortar one warming pan a long table and form a

dresser a pewter shelf a cupboard six chairs a wainscot bench one iron bar in the chimney a pair of racks a jack and three spitts valued at	07:00:00

In the Backhouse

It. one copper and brewing vessels	03:10:00

In the Great Buttery

It. 2 hogsheads one barrel and one maltquerne	01:10:00

In the Little Buttery

It. one little table a kilderkin and shelves	00:06:08

In the Dairy

It. a cheese-press a churn a cheese tub a three-footed tub and keelers some shelves and earthen ware 2 poudring tubs and bacon	03:15:00

In the Hall Chamber

It. One feather bed and bedstead with bolsters and pillows curtains and valance and blanket: 6 chairs a side-table a trunk and looking-glass all valued at	06:05:00

In the Parlour Chamber

It. one bedstead with a featherbed and bolsters and pillows curtains valance and blankets 3 great chests with linnen in them and a press-cupboard valued at	10:00:00

In the Buttery Chamber

It. one bedstead with bedding on it a chest and two chairs valued at	02:00:00

In the Cheese Chamber

It. a parcel of Cheese and shelves	01:10:00

In the Corn Chamber

It. 26 coombs of misselene* [sic] 4 coombs and 3 bushels of peas and 6 coombs of wheat	12:15:00

In the Manservants' Chamber

It. a boarded bedstead with bedding	00:10:00
It. Corn growing in the fields valued at	53:00:00
It. 11 cows 3 heifers one steer 4 burlings and 4 weanling calves valued at	29:00:00
It. 9 geldings and mares valued at	15:00:00
It. 59 sheep valued at	12:08:00

25. The Widow's Cottage, one of two charity cottages built by Robert Masters on the Green. Both have now been fully restored (see p. 130). *Photo: Jack Ravensdale*

26. Chamberlains Manor Farmhouse was originally symmetrical, but, according to local legend, an extra bay was added at a later stage to enlarge it for a twenty-first birthday party. *Photo: Jack Ravensdale*

27. The supremely elegant exterior of North Farm. *Photo: Richard Muir*

28. (*right*) View from the church tower before the field was levelled. Some of the divisions between the old peasant tenements of the Middle Ages are just visible. The splendid elm was one of the first to be lost to Dutch Elm Disease. *Photo: Jack Ravensdale*

29. (*below*) Modern farming machinery and techniques make the arable flatter than ever it was under the old open fields. *Photo: Richard Muir*

30. The hedge runs alongside the remnants of the mediaeval canal. On the left are the wharfs of Cockis Bridge, the second dock in the village. *Photo: Jack Ravensdale*

31. Part of the old Roman road towards Milton. The straightness of this section is characteristic. *Photo: Jack Ravensdale*

32. Here the Roman road has become a footpath through fields. The line can be followed on the right of the photograph. *Photo: Jack Ravensdale*

It. 6 hoggs valued at	03:00:00
It. Carts and cartgeers plows and plowgeers and other utensils of husbandry	22:01:04
It. dung in the yard valued at	01:10:00
It. fowls in the yard valued at	00:10:00
It. lumber and things forgot or not seen	00:15:00
Summa totalis	219:05:00

Fra Bland
John Taylor
Robert Taylor

*Maslin, a mixture of wheat and rye

The listing of the contents, as it is done in this inventory room by room, gives us a good idea of a house in use. The hall here is heated, and the tables and stools suggest that it is a dining-room. In the Taylor family, by this date the most substantial of the tenants, the old practice of sleeping in the hall and so taking advantage of the residual heat from the hearth, appears to have been abandoned. The house today reveals what appears to be an original fireplace in a bedroom upstairs. If this interpretation is correct, either it is unusually early, or the result of precocious pretensions.

The birding piece and traverse, which have pride of place in the hall, are very unusual in local inventories at this time. Probably the local peasantry were skilled in the use of the silent snare and the decoy, and probably also preferred sometimes to operate in undisturbed silence.

Everything about this Taylor inventory reeks of status, and the house is clearly the centre of a considerable establishment by village standards. Both butteries appear to be concerned with beer, and we do not know of another house of this period in the village which had such lavish provision.

The dairy and cheese-chamber were probably the lower and upper rooms in the old timber-framed cross-wing which has been rebuilt in brick recently. After pressing in the dairy, cheeses would be passed up through an opening in the floor to ripen in the cheese-chamber. This wing was still known as the dairy in living memory. Smaller houses in the locality usually combined their dairies and brewhouses. The Taylor establishment seems to have a brewhouse in the outshut along the back wall, the backhouse.

The existence of a manservant's chamber is probably unique up to the date of this inventory in Landbeach, but probably already represents a

33 (*right*) Typical timberwork of an eighteenth-century cottage.

34 (*below*) Roof timbers at 21, High Street. The 'wind-braces' are to give rigidity to the East Anglian type of roof which has no ridge-piece, and the strings were used by an earlier generation of thatchers to tie the first layers of thatch securely.

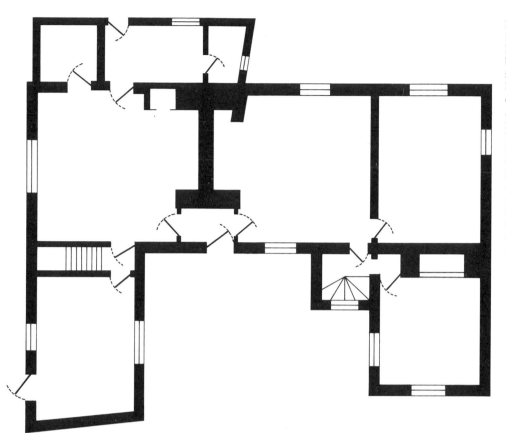

Fig. 14 Old Beach Farm is early in its use of brick for a village house in these parts. Its plan belongs to the same double-fronted family as the Plague House, but this type of plan does not often appear in brick. A tower encloses a turning newell staircase in the angle between the north wing and the hall range. The south wing was until recently a timber-framed dairy. The lean-to outshuts added along the rear wall were probably for services like a scullery, and the farmhouse kitchen could be used as a daily dining-room when the hands lived in.

division at the meal-table between farmer and servants. The chairs and table in the kitchen were probably for the employees.

Robert Taylor was a substantial mixed farmer, even having as much loose cash about him as the whole value of the estate of most small farmers in the village. One major puzzle about the use of the house remains: how was there a parlour chamber when no mention is made of a parlour? It is easy to speculate, but confirmatory evidence is not forthcoming.

Back in 1684 William Taylor had died. The farm part of the inventory, the crops and cattle are so similar to what was recorded in Robert's inventory seven years later that they must surely be substantially the same farm. But the house was much more humble. Three rooms are recorded downstairs, hall, dairy, kitchen, and three up, chamber over the kitchen, chamber over the hall, and corn chamber. Again the Taylors seem to be able to manage without disclosing a parlour. Otherwise this looks merely a slight variation on the commonest peasant house plan in

A True Inventory of the Goods &
Chattells of William Taylor of ye
Parish of Land-Beach in the County
of Cambridg: late deceased
as it was taken May 20 1684

		£ : s : d
Imprimis————	His wearing apparell & money in his purse ——	10 : 00 : 00
In the Hall ———	A Table, A Press=Cupboard a chest of drawers & other things there	02 : 00 : 00
In the Dairy ——	A Churne, A Cheespress & other things there ——	01 : 10 : 00
In the Kitchin—	Pewter & Brass, with a Copper and Brewing Vessels & other things there	06 : 00 : 00
In the Chamber over the Kitchin	Two Bedsteads with Curtains and Vallence and Bedding on them, A Trundle bed with the bedding on it, A hanging press & some other things there	10 : 00 : 00
In the Chamber over ye Hall	A Bedstead with Curtains & Vallence & Bedding on it, a chest of Linnen, a Livery Cupboard & a Wicker chaire	12 : 00 :
In the Corn Chamber	Wheat & Meslin ———————	26 : 00 : 00
In ye Reek Yard	Hay to ye Value of ten pounds ——	10 : 00 : 00
In the Yard	Eleven Mares & Goldings ———	35 : 00 : 00
In the Yard	Seventeen Milch Beasts and Eleven Gudb=Beasts ———	42 : 00 :
In the Yard	Four Swine ———————	01 : 10 :
In ye Sheepwalk	Fifty sheep & five Lambs ———	12 : 10 :
In the Stable	Cart Gears & Plow Gears, also in ye Yard Carts, Plows & other intrum.ts of Husbandry	12 : 10 : 00
In ye field	Corn upon ye ground —————	60 : 00 :
		241 :

Prized by   Robert Taylor
              John Taylor
Rivers : Taylor R his marke.

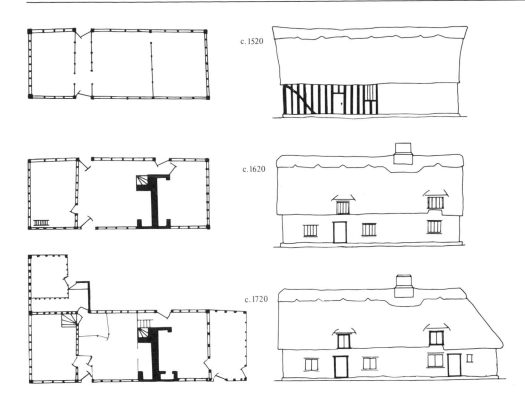

Fig. 16 This is one of the houses whose history reaches back farthest into the village past.

It was built probably at the end of the fifteenth century or in the early years of the sixteenth, as a house of three rooms, each open to the roof, and had a through passage with opposed doors. The hearth was in the middle of the floor in the central room, the hall. On either side of the fire, in each wall, are remains of mediaeval unglazed windows with diamond mullions. The room next the street seems to have been the service room where food and drink were kept and prepared. The inner room, or parlour, beyond the hearth, was a family bedroom.

Before the Civil War the accommodation was doubled by inserting the chimney and the back-to-back fireplaces, which enabled the rooms to be lofted over now that the smoke was contained by the chimney and taken away. The service room seems to have been the one lofted over first, since a ladder-like stair was fitted.

Three major alterations took place in the early eighteenth century: a lean-to was added on the rear end, probably as a dairy; a little cross-wing was built on to the front end, probably as a weaver's shed judging from the length of the window; a bread oven was inserted in the larger hearth in the parlour.

the area, the three-celled house—usually hall, parlour and kitchen with chambers above.

In the earlier of these two inventories the three apprisers are all Taylors, Robert, John and Rivers. The latter signs by mark although is found signing elsewhere. William's establishment appears very modest indeed; with the absence of parlour for dairy and corn chamber, it seems domestically poorer than the average Landbeach farmer of the time, and there seems no provision for staff, yet William's total inventory is worth even more than Robert's, chiefly in stock and crops.

*   *   *

It was quite common in this part of Cambridgeshire to find dairies being added in the eighteenth century, often as a lean-to at the lower end of the house. Most of the inventories show at least a few cattle and, with the proximity of the lush fen grass with common grazing, a specialised room was needed for dealing with the milk, and making cream, butter and cheese. Grass on the fen edge was in effect being produced from natural water meadow, and two lush crops a year were always possible in the right places. At the appropriate seasons the single and double cheeses were produced, like a fine Camembert and Stilton. It is not surprising that the dairy has such an importance that in some of the peasant houses it seems to squeeze out the parlour.

In the Taylors' inventories the indirect mention of the parlour, by reference to the chamber above it, makes us believe that there really was a parlour in the house, however oddly the appraisers had treated it, but in John Wayman's little house also, in 1686, the parlour has been ousted by a dairy. It seems to have been of the dominant type as detected by the Royal Commission on Historical Monuments, the three-celled house. It consisted of hall, kitchen and dairy, with chambers above stairs. But although this was at that time a modern house in plan, its use was well behind the times. The hall seems to have been the master bedroom, and the servants to have slept upstairs among the ripening cheese. Soon practically all bedrooms would be upstairs, and those that were not are likely, in probate inventories, to have been due to making up a sick-bed in which to nurse the master of the house downstairs.

But new fashion in building did not take over all at once in a single generation. As time went by old houses would be modernised to conform to current standards, while new houses would rarely imitate the old, even when a cheap, mean job was done.

William Baldin's inventory has crumbled at the edges so that the valuations are no longer there for some detailed items. It presents an old-fashioned appearance for 1681. His kitchen, certainly, is a place for the preparation of food, even if it contains three chamber pots. The hall doubles as principal bedroom and main reception room. The buttery seems to be such in name only, it being a rough second bedroom. The valuation figure for the whole of his goods and chattels is intact, just over fourteen pounds. The whole document suggests that he was a very poor man, getting most of his living from the common rights that went with his house. He was running nineteen sheep in the Sheepwalk with the help of 'a little old horse' in his yard, and with a pig to supply some winter meat. The type of house in which he lived, with all its rooms on the ground floor, ceased to be built, even in the remoter fens, about the time of the Reformation. Thereafter, even if they were small and poky, at the very least there would be some sort of attic. By 1681, most of those that still survived had had a chimney and floor inserted, thus immediately doubling the number of rooms, and from what we have seen of William Baldin's house, such a change must have been most welcome to the householder.

Landbeach seems to have a private bias of its own in that where there are three-celled houses in the Restoration period, in Landbeach they seem much more likely to have a dairy as the third ground-floor room than in neighbouring villages where the word parlour is more likely. William Baldin was old-fashioned in the whole style of his house, as well as the usage of room names. John Wayman, however, was using the new type of house in an old-fashioned way and, unlike William Baldin, his farming stock shows him to have been a man of substance. He owned horses and cattle but his main asset was a flock of 90 sheep, and his pastoral interests predominated over arable. The family name was one of the longest-lasting in Landbeach, surviving in the village and surrounding district until living memory. What inventories never tell us, of course, is whether the house is as built or whether it has been modernised to current fashion.

35 This eighteenth-century cottage has responded delightfully to sensitive restoration.

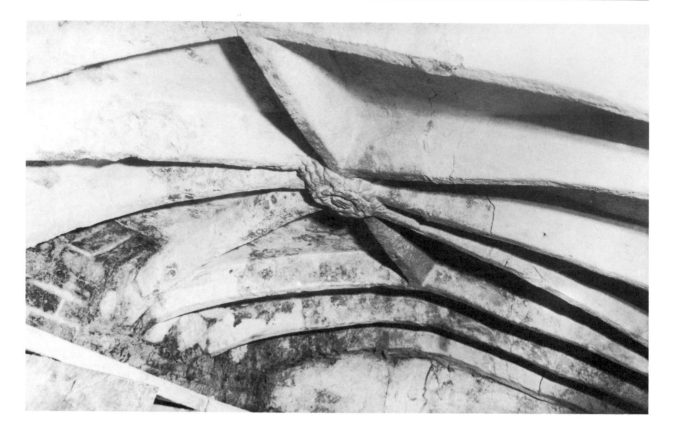

36 The Rectory: the ceiling of the fourteenth-century cellar.

37 (*opposite page*) The Rectory: 'Screens Passage' and Jacobean panelling.

The oldest house or part of a house to survive in Landbeach today is the cellar in Landbeach House, the former Rectory. This has a fourteenth-century rib-vaulted ceiling with carved stone bosses and coats of arms of the bishops de Lisle and Arundel, which confirm the dating. It was shortened in one of the many rebuildings, and the access stairs were then moved to the opposite end. Previously it had been reached from a passageway which ran round the east end of the house as a projecting cross-wing. The dramatic picture which strikes anyone coming in from the rear court through the back door is of a perpendicular arcade, decorated with fleurons and a niche for an image. At first sight this looks like a stone screen, originally between a hall, or pseudo-hall, and a service wing.

Building operations and restoration a few years ago demonstrated that the wing where the rector and curate had rooms in the early leases was of red brick, and that the moulded arches and decorations were stucco over the rubbed red brick foundation. The upper storeys and the rest of the house are timber-framed, with a brick skin added in various areas at different times, until the whole of the exterior shows brick.

The man who reconstructed the house from its mediaeval pattern was

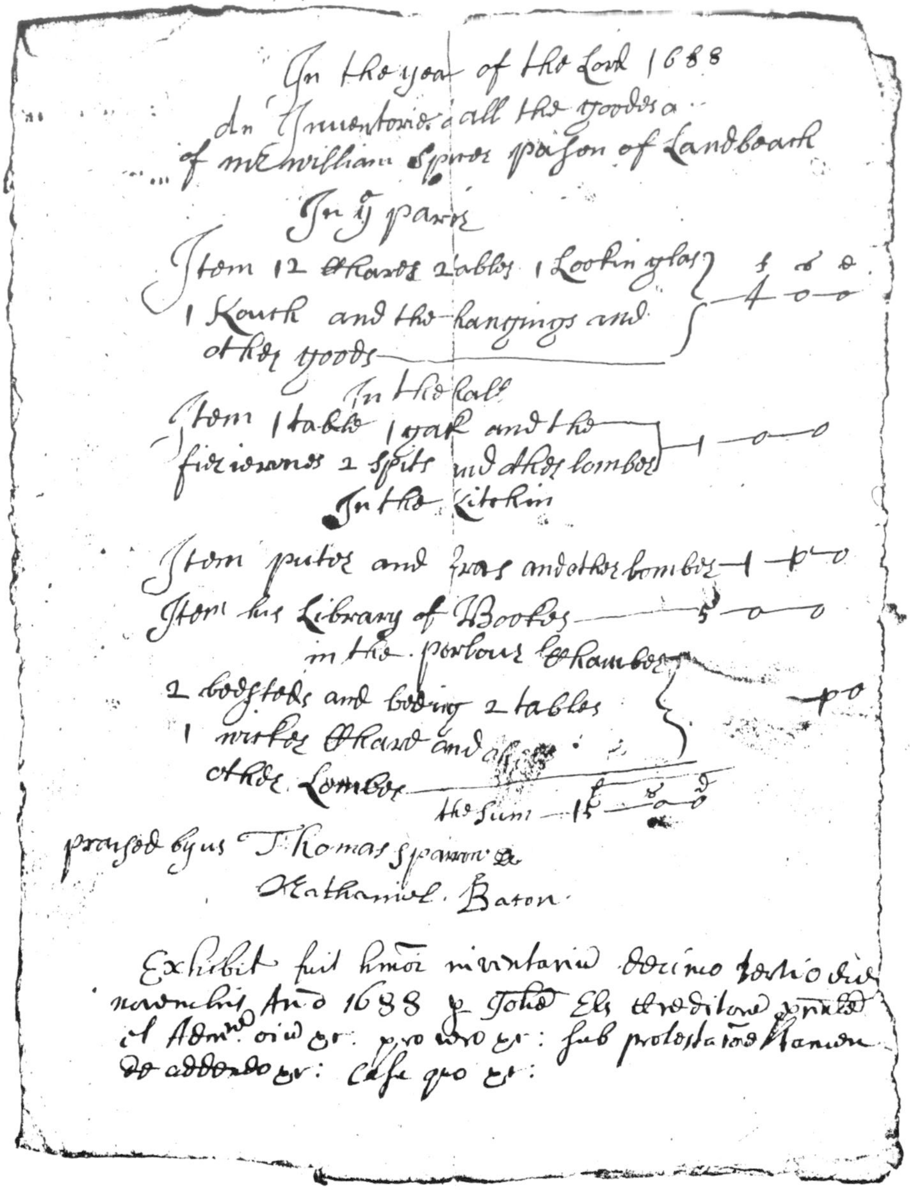
In the year of the Lord 1688
An Inventorie of all the goods
of Mr William Spencer parson of Landbeach
In the parlor
Item 12 chairs 2 tables 1 Looking glass
1 Couch and the hangings and
other goods
In the hall
Item 1 table 1 jack and the
fire irons 2 spits and other lumber — 1 0 0
In the kitchin
Item pewter and brass and other lumber — 1
Item his Library of Books — 5 0 0
in the parlour chamber
2 bedsteds and bedding 2 tables
1 winter chair and other
other Lumber
the sum — 15
prased by us Thomas Sparrow
Nathaniel Baron
Exhibit fuit hmoi inventariu decimo tertio die
novembris Ano 1688 ...

Fig. 17 The probate inventory of Mr William Spencer, parson of Landbeach in 1688. His library books were assessed in a lump sum at five pounds. *By permission of the Syndics of Cambridge University Library.*

William Sowode, rector 1528–44. He complained of the amount that he had spent on the house, and regretted that he would never see the full value of his money again.

The roof of the cellar now projects in an extraordinary style, and it could well represent the line of an aisle of a former mediaeval hall. This speculation becomes more forceful when one looks at Masters' drawing of the front elevation of the house as it came down to him, where the front door is placed at the end of a passage which could represent the aisle on the other side of the former hall from the cellar. Sowode's rebuilding seems to have reduced the earlier Rectory, an aisled hall, by removing its aisles, and converting the remainder into a clergy house.

38 The Rectory: this chimney on the east side of the Great Hall was the work of William Sowode shortly before Matthew Parker became rector.

To this a substantial farmhouse was added with pseudo-hall range and one cross-wing. The brick hearth and the chimney with crow-stepped gables would be typical of Sowode's time. Early in the first wave of sixteenth-century rebuilding, it incorporated mediaeval tradition with something to raise the standard of domestic comfort.

Sowode's rectory was a better house than would have been needed by a largely absentee rector who carried out his parish duties mainly through curates. It was much improved for a resident rector, and when Matthew Parker arrived, to become our first married rector with a family, it probably had more to recommend it, even though Parker's stays were probably relatively brief.

39 The Rectory: moulded beams and joints in the ceiling of the Great Hall.

40 (*opposite page*) The Rectory: part of Robert Masters' grand entrance hall and staircase.

In 1746, when Robert Masters became rector, the house was modified and up-dated to suit a country gentleman. He enclosed the space between the two front wings to take in space for an impressive entrance hall, with a grand staircase rising to the balcony and landing, by the library and drawing-room. The old hall was degraded to a kitchen. The back of the old house now became the front elevation. Sash windows replaced the old Tudor mullions, and the whole conformed with the new insistence on symmetry by including a false blind sash in the end of the Little Parlour, invisible inside, but externally providing the extra window needed for balance.

Masters' son-in-law, T. C. Buroughes, made further additions enhancing the Rectory as country house. By this time William Worts had bequeathed the manor of Brays to the University and the rector from now on, having to be resident, could double for squire. John Tinkler added a second storey to the bay-window that Burroughes had added to the Little Parlour, running it right up to the eaves, and installed the Renaissance-style stone front porch. The new rooms created by this group of parsons were brilliantly conceived and executed with perfect taste.

To this 'Country House for an English Gentleman' was added a garden to match. What the Middle Ages had known as Parson's Cowyard became

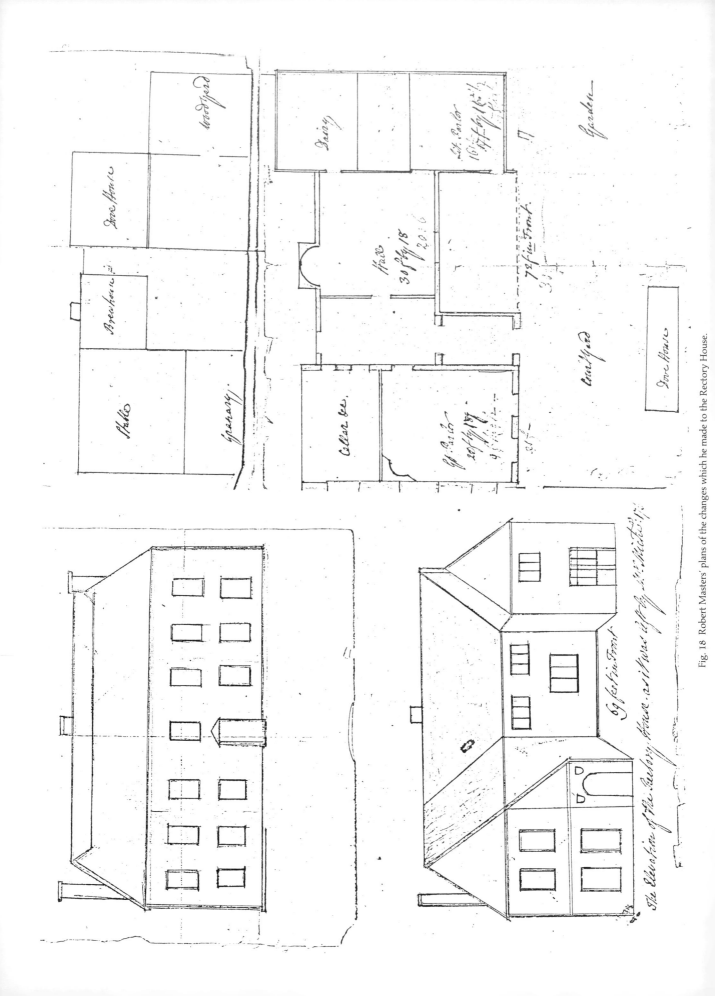

Fig. 18 Robert Masters' plans of the changes which he made to the Rectory House.

a pleasure ground. A circular gravelled drive for carriages led through the walled garden to the grand front door. In time the bay-trees filled its centre and towered over the house. Walks were changed and new lawns laid down.

Burroughes left behind a meticulous account of his new plantings. There were peaches and nectarines, and ornamental trees that would have done credit in an aristocratic park:

Six Cedars of Libanus and ten Red Cedars, Arbutus and Arbor Vitae.

Shrubberies were set up with twelve Portugal Laurels.

Six Pyracanthas, ten Junipers and ten Swedish Junipers.

Some of the few giants that survived into recent years could have been of Burroughes' planting in their extreme old age.

The Rectory was not simply the finest house in the village; it dominated it. But in the year of Waterloo all this was threatened, not by Bonaparte's troops, but by the property next door to the parson.

July 11th 1815

Revd Sir,

The following subject is of so much importance to me and my successors in the Rectory of Landbeach that I have lost no time in acquainting you with it.

I have just heard from good authority that Mr Hemington's small estate consisting of about one acre of land with a little grove of elm trees on it —a cottage and a barn both in a dilapidated state adjoining to the Rectory garden are now to be disposed of—that a person is in treaty for the purchase, a higless in the trade of fatting geese for the London market, a trade of all others the most offensive, creating a horrid stench with a continued clangour night and day for ten months in the year. Should this take place it will entail a nuisance intolerable to all the present and future inhabitants of the rectory-house, for I find the trade of such a nature that it usually descends in the same family from one generation to another and there are already two families closely related to each other following the same trade in great annoyance of everyone who lives near them in this parish. There is now one goosery within 500 yards of us which with a south wind is frequently very offensive to us.

The most prompt measures only can prevent this threatening evil, as I understand the man is anxious to get possession at Michaelmas next—

I have not been upon visiting terms with Mr Hemington for many years and therefore I cannot flatter myself with hopes of any personal accommodation from him, but with humble submission to your judgement I think your tenant Hall might be a proper agent upon the occasion.

127

Poor Mr Wilkinson who was fully acquainted with all the circumstances attached to this business had often assured me it was his wish that the Society should again consent to the purchase as soon as opportunity might offer, although their design and proposals had been before rejected by the owner of the estate.

It is an object so important to my comfort as well as that of future rectors that I cannot refrain from entreating you with the consent of the Society to show me this indulgence in addition to that patronage which I have been proud to acknowledge with the finest sense of gratitude.

I am, Revd Sir, with much
esteem Yr obliged and obedient
T. C. Burroughes

To Revd Dr. Douglas.

Dr Douglas was the Master of Corpus Christi at that time. Burroughes seems to have had his way.

Whether the Rectory was being considered as a farmhouse or country gentleman's residence, it needed a substantial staff to run an establishment of that size. Plenty of servants could be accommodated in the attics, from which they could pass unseen and unheard down the narrow back stairs to the kitchen (Matthew Parker's Great Hall). Cottages on the Green were provided for a married coachman and other living-out servants.

These continued the tradition, but in a different style, of the cottages that Masters had built for a parish clerk and a schoolmistress or poor widow. A recent restoration of the Widow's Cottage exposed Masters' initials: 'RM' in wrought iron on the gable end on either side of the chimney. The cottage was one of the smaller patterns common in the eighteenth century, but with concessions to the use of one room as a schoolroom for a girls' Sunday School. It had two rooms on the ground-floor with tiniest attics above, three windows to the front looking on to the street, and a nicely panelled front door, with an opposed one at the rear. There was a small fireplace with a small square flue at either gable end, very much in the favourite cottage style of the time.

The Clerk's Cottage, before the recent fire and restoration, was a little gem of a memorial to a very particular phase of English sensibility. It was again single storied, but quite symmetrical with hipped gable and central chimney stacks above back-to-back fireplaces. There is a straight joint where the brickwork emerges from the roof, suggesting that the second fireplace may have been a later addition.

Inside a frame of wooden classical pilasters and pediment was a panelled front door. Both the pediment and the upper panels of the door

41 (*above*) Skachbow cottage, one of the houses on the Green. The axial chimney points to a seventeenth-century origin.

42 (*left*) The interior of Skachbow, showing the dressed stone which, like the foundations of Old Beach Farmhouse, probably came from the mediaeval manor house of Chamberlains. Several other houses on the Green also made use of this source of stone.

were decorated with fourteenth-century carved woodwork that Masters took from the church, probably from the screen made redundant when he pulled down the dilapidated Lady Chapel to make the church symmetrical, as all proper buildings should be at that time.

The cottage as he left it was a strange monument to the English Romantic Revival, a small *cottage orné*, with classic and Gothic elements not fighting but in complete unity. The axial chimney looked back to the earlier tradition of the first generation of cottages that had a chimney. When it was built, contemporary fashion would have put the flues to the

43 The Clerk's Cottage, built on the Green by Robert Masters, now restored after being gutted by fire. Its companion, the Widow's Cottage, can be seen in colour picture 25

gable ends. So the vernacular became classical in its symmetrical placing of all the elements of the building. This axial chimney has every appearance from the outside of belonging to an age earlier than Robert Masters, and it was already being suggested while his widow and son-in-law were still alive that he had restored, not built, the cottage, and therefore had no right to 'give and devize' to his son-in-law and his heirs any of the three cottages which he had built on the Green. He was relying on the right of the lord of the soil, the lord of the manor, to 'approve' part of the 'waste' for such a purpose. In his own hand there is a small document written on both sides:

> Copy of an Act of the Chapter of the Master and Fellows of Benet College [Corpus Christi College] dated 16th February 1791.
>
> Mr Masters having signified his intention of appropriating a cottage at Landbeach, which now he holds of the manor of Chamberlains to the use of the Clerk of the Parish, it is agreed (as far as by law we may) to renew the copy as often as it shall become vacant without fine or fee, on condition that the quit rent which is now four pence a year, be advanced to one shilling a year.

The dorse of the document seems to tell us something of the social relations in the village at that time.

> We, the inhabitants of Landbeach do thankfully accept the accommodation on the other side and further consent and agree to appropriate the piece of ground adjoining to the south end of the said cottages to the same purpose without demanding any rent for the same.
>
> Apr.29 1791   Robert Masters, Rector   John Foote
>   Francis Tingay   Uriah Taylor
>   Wm Wilson   John Hall

It is tempting to speculate on the gap between the College formally agreeing, and the villagers, led by their rector, signing. It hardly suggests that the acceptance was spontaneous. Nor does the villagers' bad law make Masters' better. Masters would surely have liked to be the lord of the manor; he seems to have had difficulty in realising that he was not. Domesday might have found him hard to contain had he lived then.

Masters is probably the person responsible for the survival of a number of Poor Law documents in the parish archives since most of the collection is from his period, and many of them he has signed as JP. Until the nineteenth century brought fireproof safes, all archives were kept in the parish chest in the church.

The first of those still surviving is from 1787. It is a settlement certificate for a widow and her ten-month-old baby, who have come from Waterbeach. Some of the family seem to have followed at some stage and descendants are still here. Parallel certificates to allow Waterbeach people to work in Landbeach without the parish becoming legally responsible for them are the most common among those in the chest, and a number are from Cottenham, Milton and other nearby villages. There is a removal order to send one pauper back to Hertfordshire. Slightly later there is a bastardy order which seems to take advantage of the fact that the putative father is a yeoman. He has to pay 18s. for maintenance up to the time of the order, and 2s. a week thereafter. He has to find £1 for confinement expenses and 6s. for obtaining the affiliation order. The mother has to pay 1s. per week, 'in case she shall not nurse and take care of the child herself'.

11

Running the Village:
Manor and Vestry

Early in the Tudor period the parish, with new machinery and new officers, began to take power in village affairs, but Landbeach is one of those villages where the manor long retained importance. As long as villagers farmed the land and the lord collected rents, he had a strong interest in regulation and control. Sometimes the two lords, or their officers, worked together. Sometimes they seem to have failed to do this but to have rectified it with afterthoughts.

Orders by Thomas Cosyn and William Raccliffe have survived from 1498, representing the lordships of Chamberlains and Brays. There are two sets from the troubled year of 1549 when Kirby came near to civil war against the Chamberlains tenants, and some of the provisions seem aimed at him. Both seem to have come from the Chamberlains court. One is headed:

> The verdict of the 12 men Anno Edwardi Sexti 2ndo
> within this lordship [sic: inserted as second thought?]

First that every copyholder repair their tenement and house in thacking between this day and Our Lady Day in Lent upon pain of 13s.4d. and to repair them in timber work between this and Lammas upon pain of 6s.8d.

That every man sufficiently make and repair their houses in hedging ditching and walling between neighbour and neighbour upon pain of forfeit for every pole 12d. between this and St Andrew's Day next.

That every man for their portion scour their ditches and common drains as well within the towns as in the fields between this and St

Andrew's Day upon pain of forfeiting for any acre 4d. ~~so that the lord do the same~~ [sic]

That every man for their portion make the ditch in the Furfen called Tillage between this and Christmas next upon pain for forfeiting for every acre 12d. ~~so the lord do the same~~ [sic]

Item that Thomas Mooreshall leave selling of ale and other victuals before this St Andrew's Day upon pain of 3s.4d.

Item Robert Parsey for selling ale by small measures 1d.

Item Thomas Mitton for the same 1d.

Item Robert Lane of Cambridge baker for selling small bread.

Item William Baker of Chesterton for the same 2d.

Item that every man keep their hogs within hogroots and in no other place upon pain of forfeiting.

There is what seems to be another version of most of this on undated vellum in Latin and a similar set from the leet.

Landbeach Ordinances and pains made there at the court and leet holden the second day of November in anno Regni Regis Edwardi Sexti Secundo.

First it is ordained that no tenant or inhabitant of the aforesaid town shall keep upon the commons there above the number of three sheep for an acre under pain to forfeit to the lord 20d.

Item it is ordained that no tenant shall take in to feed upon the commons of this town the sheep of any stranger above two sheep for an acre and to take of the lord's farmer there for every acre upon pain to forfeit 40d.

Item it is ordained by the homage that every copyholder of this lordship shall repair the tenements and houses in thacking before Our Lady Day next coming upon pain of forfeiting 13s.4d. and to repair them in timber before Lammas next upon pain of 6s.8d.

Item that every tenant for their parts scour their common drains and watercourses as well within the town as in the field before the feast of St Nicholas next coming upon pain to forfeit for every acre 4d. and the lord's farmer to make his part. Item it is ordained that every tenant make his part and portion in the ditch of Furfen called Tillage before Christmas next upon pain to forfeit for every acre 12d. and the lord's farmer to make his part.

Item it is commanded and ordained that John Utton and John Royton to repair their tenements and houses sufficiently being now very ruinous as well for lack of timber as thack before the Feast of the Nativity of Our Lord God next coming upon pain to forfeit their lands and tenements.

Also it is ordained that Thomas Moore shall leave selling of ale and other victuals before St Andrew's Day next upon pain to forfeit 3s.4d.

Also it is commanded to Henry Edwards that he pay his rent now being behind before the feast of the Nativity of Our Lord next upon pain to forfeit his lands and tenement.

Already by the time of the Hundred Rolls many local manors, and that of Chamberlains among them, had been given, or had usurped, the right to hold the Assize of Bread and Ale. This is usually regarded as early consumer regulation, but at the time was regarded as a perquisite like the profits of justice, the income generated by fines and confiscations of a court.

Ale-tasters, whose job it was to test the quality of each brew, were appointed at most courts and fined for not doing their job at the next. This still puzzles students of the mediaeval manor. More comprehensible was the fining of brewers and bakers, who had been licensed at court, with unfailing regularity at subsequent courts for selling ale or bread below standard, or selling ale in cups instead of properly stamped measures. Bakers would be fined for giving short weight, and those who took in paying guests would be fined for doing so.

The concept of licensing hours has a long history. Taverns were to stop serving and close when curfew rang and the fire was covered. It is interesting to see how centuries of practice seem to leave us with the manor court enforcing a simplified and more sensible Assize of Bread and Ale. But the idea of public duty in private hands is somewhat out of place in 1549.

Agricultural regulation in that year, not surprisingly in view of the struggle against Kirby, is dominated by the stinting of the numbers of sheep, not least 'foreign' sheep brought in from nearby villages. At this stage the lord still has full common rights, and his allowance of sheep in the commons is fifty per cent above that of the tenants. The landlord's interest as a receiver of rents tended in time to become more important than his interests in cultivation. Correspondingly his attention was more and more devoted to repair and maintenance. A large number of timber-framed buildings with thatched roofs would mean that the lord or his officers could never let up. House repairs are usually ordered very specifically, thatch needing regular repair, and after thatch the most common fault seems rotten groundsills, the long timbers laid horizontally on the plinths and to which the vertical studs were fixed. Closest to the damp soil, groundsills were (and are) the first to go.

A point of interest in this particular set of ordinances for repairs is the

44 (*above*) The Plague House after restoration. Compare with colour pictures 19 and 20.

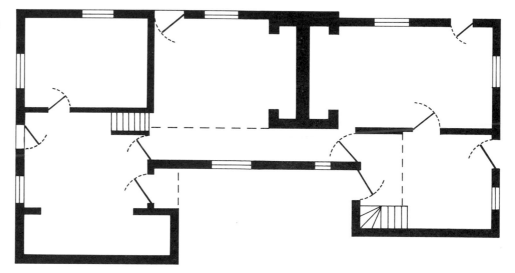

Fig. 19 Like Old Beach Farm, the Plague House is a local example of the double-fronted family of house plans from the Middle Ages and after. It is timber-framed and in part mediaeval. Ceilings in the hall and parlour were installed when the back-to-back fireplaces were inserted in two stages against, and then replacing, an earlier through-passage. The aisle-like passage at the rear was probably added as an 'outshut' when the new fireplaces would otherwise have blocked all access from the parlour to the rest of the house.

difference in time allowed to comply. The more difficult job of replacing timber was allowed a long hot summer, where thatchers would work with wet straw anyway and would not expose so much of the interior and contents of the house to bad weather.

Ditching was always one of the major problems as seen through orders and manor court rolls, at least until the great drainage of the fens.

In the course of the sixteenth century the problem of poverty, both of the infirm through age or sickness, and the workless vagrant, the sturdy beggar, got out of hand. Tudor governments, with little success, stumbled along in the wake of the pioneering towns, trying to create work for the sturdy, and to stir up, channel and control alms-giving. In the past the manor had, by custom, in-built systems of poor relief. In some cases, where a single heir would inherit all, provision of some sort had to be made for a widow and siblings. In Landbeach retiring villeins should normally have had a third of the house and some provision for maintenance. The increase of the population outside the shelter of any kind of inheritance; itinerant bands of beggars, re-inforced by discharged soldiers after each foreign war, and by 'dissolute serving-men' every time the keeping of private armies was discouraged; or when new-fashioned landlords failed to maintain hospitality and large households—all this contributed to the fear of governments at the vagabond menace in years of discontent, or the terror in Westminster from beggars in time of plague. They expected the churchwardens in each parish to put a finger in the dyke and hold back the flood. These were to appoint two collectors in each parish who should 'gently ask' alms for the relief of the poor. This was to stem the flood of distress caused as much as anything by the inflation and debasement of the currency generated by government over-spending, especially on defence.

The government moved with hesitation and reluctance to making poor rates compulsory: alms-giving attracted merit to the giver. Contemporary morality was dubious of doles. In the hope of retaining the virtues of Christian charity, those who were unwilling could be subjected to a course of sermons. At first, those who could work should have jobs provided for them. The able-bodied who would not take work if offered were encouraged by whipping, branding and enslaving. Under Elizabeth I the more sensible of the measures were encoded into a practical system which left the responsibility fairly and squarely on the shoulders of the parish, but gave it the power to raise necessary rates.

The earlier phase of poor relief in Landbeach is commemorated for us by a little pewter alms dish from the days of gentle asking. Its inscription, 'For the towne of Landbeach', exactly matches that on the beautifully damascened chalice.

Charitable bequests meant that the parson and overseers of the poor, who normally included the churchwardens, would have to cope with capital and interest as well as payment of expenses. Bound up in the first register book (whose entries begin at the first date of the national system in 1538) are churchwardens' and vestry accounts. A very important part in a village with commons and fens on the scale of Landbeach was to elect field officers with a sphere of operations extending over all the village and not just a single manor. Records of such elections, hiring of herds and swineherds, and appointment of minor field officers, survive from 1651 for a number of years.

The first note of the choosing of a swineherd in 1651, as far as the entry can be deciphered, seems to indicate payment in kind. The cowherd gets payment in cash, 3d. per quarter for a milch cow, and for beasts of

45 The village as it is today, a long, curving High Street making a series of vistas. Number 34, the house nearest the camera, can be seen before restoration in colour picture 22.

agistment 2d. per quarter, '. . . and he is to have two cows to go for this year upon the commons'. In the following year supernumerary appointments were made: 'Jo Patten is hired at the same time for one year to fill the moules in . . . High Fen and to spread the dung there. He is to have six shillings and to be free of common day work'.

A horsekeeper in the High Fen was also to look after Frith Fen at wages of 5d. per week.

The 'hoggard', William Whitworth, was to have 4d. per quarter for every hog for two quarters.

The herd, Henry Tiplady, employed his son as assistant: 'Henry Tiplady's boy is to help him keep cows there for three quarters, and he is to have for his services ten shillings a quarter paid to him by his father, the said money to be put into the hands of Mr Barnes to be paid to the said boy as he shall think convenient, and the boy is to have meat, drink, lodging and walking periods provided him by his father.' The use of a servant by the herd was normal, and although, in this instance, the father needed watching, the re-engagement of a herd in 1681 included this obligation: '. . . and to bring the cattle at home at night and to leave no cattle behind at night and to blow his horn every morning and to be careful in fetching up the cattle in our own bounds at Michaelmas time and to hire a substantial boy to help him to keep the herd and to be kind to him; and his own beasts to go free in the Common and Meadow.'

There was a different kind of transaction recorded in this period. Four acres of town land were regularly let for a cash rent with an obligation for dunging at ten loads an acre. In 1653 the dunging had not been mentioned.

More delicate still for parish officers was the use and care of capital assets. On December 23rd, 1671, Robert Taylor borrowed £4:5:6d., being part of the charitable bequest made in 1609 by John Vipers ('Old Vipers' as he was known) for the poor. One hopes that the poor found the rate of interest modest. Robert Taylor, William Annis, and Francis Gonnell, the farmers mentioned as borrowing the capital of the Trust, were what contemporaries usually styled, the 'most substantiallest' of the village. In his *History of the Parish of Landbeach* (Cambridge, 1861), W. K. Clay has an eloquent silence: 'the whole sum covered by these entries is £5:15:04d. The money has long since disappeared.'

The work of parochial officers in local government was increasingly controlled by JPs in Quarter Sessions, and the records show them overseeing the local housing development on behalf of the poor. Governments had long been convinced that much evil flowed from houses without any field land going with them, Elizabeth's so-called 'Cottage Act' of 1589 banned the building of houses with less than four acres of land attached

46 A modern boost to the village in a seventeenth-century setting. The portrait head is of Dr J. N. McArthur of McArthur Microscopes, who brought scientific technology to Landbeach without changing the landscape. The brain centre for the new industry is the tastefully restored Skachbow cottage.

and forbade the division of cottages or the taking in of lodgers. The Justices were allowed to exempt cottages intended for the poor.

Minutes of Quarter Sessions, Easter 1666:
. . . one cottage lately erected and built, wherein Smith, a poor, lame, aged and impotent person now liveth, shall stand and be continued for the habitation and dwelling of the said William Smith and not longer according to the Statute in that case provided, 31 Eliz. I.

There follows the like order for seven more poor people's cottages including that of William Wells.

There is another version in the College with one significant difference: Elizabeth Wells, widow, appears instead of William Wells.

We are not likely to be surprised when one of a list of aged poor dies in the brief space while a petition is waiting for a routine endorsement, but this is the time when, according to local legend, two old ladies ran away from the Plague in London and came to Landbeach, to the house since called the Plague House, only for it to become apparent that they had brought it with them. The popular form of the legend reports that no one in the village, apart from the parson and his family, would go near them, and that the parson, his family and servants all died. Certainly the rector's son died, and father's handwriting over the next eighteen months suggests that he was shattered by the happenings, and sank, a broken man disintegrating steadily, through his final year and a half.

The Elizabethan ban on taking in lodgers was a natural result of the terror produced by plague. Beggars also could probably spread infected fleas as fast as could the rats.

One of the names of the poor admitted to a cottage by the Quarter Sessions was none other than Henry Tiplady, the herd with the assistant son. Even after paying the boy he should have had adequate income from the post of village herd. Even his son was not doing too badly— 30/- was not a bad year's wage so long as it was in fact paid to the boy and not the father, and that his food and lodging were provided, as they should have been by his father. We are tantalised, and left with a mystery as to the habits of Tiplady senior.

12

Village School and Chapel: Establishment and Dissent

Buried in the churchwardens' accounts are two payments referring to a school in Landbeach: in 1639 a payment for mending the school house, and in 1650 for restoring it. In her book *Contrasting Communities* (Cambridge, 1974), Dr Margaret Spufford included Landbeach in her list of villages with a continuous history of schooling since 1575. It may, of course, go back much earlier, even to the Cambridge Humanists at the beginning of the sixteenth century.

William Gonnell, friend of Erasmus, had a house at the north end of the village. Erasmus kept a horse in his paddock, and would come and stay when plague broke out in Cambridge. At one stage, Gonnell seems to have had a school where North Farm now stands. Later he became tutor to Thomas More's children. It is quite possible that it is from his school that the one we hear of later sprang.

In 1727 Bishop Greene's Description of the Diocese showed that a public school for reading and writing had just been erected. When Masters became rector in 1746 the school was held in the Lady Chapel, then in a most dilapidated condition: it had been held there at least as far back as 1687. Masters, as we have seen, pulled it down to make the East end of the church more symmetrical, and made other arrangements for school and teacher in his charity buildings on the Green.

In 1868, to secure the future of a Church of England school, the present Old School buildings were put up by public subscription. It is a very simple attempt to make a Victorian version of Gothic vernacular, a hall and cross-wing, with nothing fancy and completely at home in the heart of the village.

47 (*opposite page*) North Farm, magnificently from the Age of Elegance, where William Gonnell had his school and entertained Erasmus.

The whole was put up by two brothers Unwin in six weeks.

Under the new act of Parliament it had some difficulty in keeping going. Her Majesty's Inspectors made demands as a price of declaring it efficient. They insisted on it being enlarged to take eighty instead of sixty pupils, in anticipation of compulsory attendance (it never needed more than sixty places). The single buttress shows where it was extended very skilfully and unobtrusively with the windows just right.

The Inspectors were shocked because the children sat at chairs and tables. They could never allow the school to be efficient unless parallel-sided desks were provided. The battle to have the teacher, Miss Jane Smith, certified efficient, was long-drawn-out. She was the daughter of the turnkey at Cambridge gaol. It is not clear that there was any sound reason why the HMI did not visit and certify her, as they had power to do. The correspondence has a slightly sulphurous smell. The Church was back to the wall in that it could not supply sufficient certificated teachers overnight where it had been managing for years with most of its force uncertificated. There would appear to have been guerrilla war between the Church and the Board of Education. But Miss Smith studied part-time and took her examination. All was well.

At the time of the Domesday, what little education existed was completely in the hands of the Church—at least, this was true of all formal education. While there still was a school in Landbeach, the church always had great power in it. Some parsons interpreted their duties at the school quite liberally. For example, two boys were seen by the rector knocking conkers off the trees in the churchyard. Out came his notebook, down went their names, and the next morning, as a start to the school day, he presented himself to call them out and cane them. Fifty years ago this was regarded as normal and right.

The closing of the school in 1965 was only at the end of a fifteen-year battle. Twenty years on, we wonder if the closure would have been possible at all if delayed until now. Its loss seems more plainly each year to have cost the village dear in its cohesion and sense of purpose. Radical educational changes seem to come in brash packages. When the school was finally closed in the teeth of local opinion it was explained that it was necessary to allow efficient streaming and proper team games. Educational doctrine seems to have adopted the rapid rate of turn-over from older and wiser beliefs.

In religious life the parish church did not have everything quite so much its own way. There had been little sign of early Dissent, only one in 1676, but in 1816 a Baptist chapel was erected at the southern end of the village. It seated 150 persons, but by the middle of the century it needed replacement. The present chapel was built in 1854, and the old

48 (*right*) Georgian taste lingers on at North Farm.

49 (*below*) The Baptist Chapel balances the sturdy classical exterior with elegant use of cast-iron in window frames, slender pillars supporting the galleries and delicate balustrades. It has survived remarkably unspoilt.

one, in spite of the graves under the floor, became a granary and a gig-house.

The new chapel, Classical in style, just a few years younger than Crystal Palace, had the latest in window frames, cast-iron, and is faintly reminiscent of the great iron and glass palace. Inside cast-iron is used even more elegantly, with slender pillars supporting the gallery, and cast plant forms used to carry the mahogany hand rails right up to the organ. The box pews have only recently gone in favour of chairs. Only recently, too, have the panels of the gallery been stripped back to the bare pine, which looks exactly right in proportion to the rest of the building.

But times move, even for church and chapel buildings. Electric lighting had to come to replace the original oil lamps, and electric heaters replaced the old solid fuel stove. In spite of these comforts and conveniences one can feel that few essentials have changed since this new chapel was first built.

Here often came the great preacher Spurgeon, who at eighteen had been pastor of Waterbeach Baptist Church. Once he had to stand across the road in a cart to preach because the crowd was otherwise too great to hear him.

The Baptists had a special reason for pride when, at a General Election, they opened their doors to a Liberal who was also a Jew, after the Church School managers had refused him the use of the school for a meeting.

13

Drainage, Navigation and Enclosure

The richness of the soil on the fen edge made it a tempting place for anyone who could get rid of the water, to make his fortune. Compared with its neighbours, Landbeach had relatively little ground that flooded every winter, and when serious attempts to drain the fens began in the early seventeenth century, Landbeach began to show early results. In an early Book of Sewers (drainage minutes and other records) we can read a survey of the village as part of a general view of the land near the River Ouse:

> Landbeach hath a ground called High Fen alias Cowpasture, divided from Denney Pastures with a hedge and ditch and there is sometimes, in some parts of the winter a dozen acres or thereabouts overflown with the water that cometh out of Milton fields, Landbeach fields, Impington, Histon and Cottenham fields, when their arable lands are exceedingly drowned with great rains, and an acre so overflowed is worth twenty shillings per annum.
>
> Item: the inhabitants of Landbeach are forced to be at great charges in the summer time to scour ponds and make pits to open springs in the lower part of the said fen to get water for their cattle for want whereof they stand stade (?) divers years of late great loss by the death of their cattle.

At the same time, in the next village, Cottenham, where they had very extensive wet fens, they were complaining that recent draining and embanking had forced them in the dry summers to put barn doors in the ditches to hold the water and send it back into the fields and meadows. This was in 1618.

There is in the parish records of Landbeach a seventeenth-century handwritten book dealing mainly with the sharing out of the grass grown for hay in the meadow grounds. The width of the strips had been reduced by shortening the rod with which they were measured from sixteen to thirteen feet, so leaving an unallocated area of grass which was then sold as the church lots to defray church rates. Two men were paid regularly for 'carrying a rope in the fen', as part of the laying out process. Each year this began at what had been the end in the previous year. In this way everyone had some variety in his grass crop and a better chance of being pleased.

Important in the management of the meadow grounds was the water supply and drainage, and so it is that this fen book carries the jury's account of the history of Beach Lode:

> That the old men, inhabitants of Landbeach, say and depose upon their conscience that a certain ditch called Lode Ditch, lying between the High Fen and the ground of Denney, stretching from the south-west corner of Denney Closes, by the side of the said High Fen of Landbeach unto the north-east corner of Frith Fen, was never scoured or made of duty, nor as no defence lawful for any cattle between ground and ground; but the inhabitants made the ditch at their own liberty and will to drain their common pasture from water falling and draining into Tilling and so from Tilling to run forth into the fens in the foresaid ditch called Lode Ditch; for at that time were more wetter and moist years than are now at this present time.

Part of the movement of water in the fen was seasonal. This was the annual change as winter came on and the black waters seeped up through the peat, and the water level rose, until spring brought the ebb and lowering again. It was in winter time that the barge traffic moved more freely. The other variation, the sudden and extraordinary flood, came with heavy or prolonged rain on the hills of the vast catchment area, when the white waters from the upland hurried down in spate, far more than the rivers and drains could take, or that the outfalls could let out to the sea. This could create conditions such as were described by the surveyors early in the seventeenth century. The Ouse they mention is scarcely recognisable as our Old West River, so docile that it will flow in either direction by opening or closing a sluice gate:

> Certain sudden crooks, turnings and windings of the River Ouse, especially between the fenny grounds of Cottenham and Wilburton . . . not only very dangerous unto navigators and watermen in times of storms and tempests, but also great and notorious hindrance to the fall and descent of the waters . . .

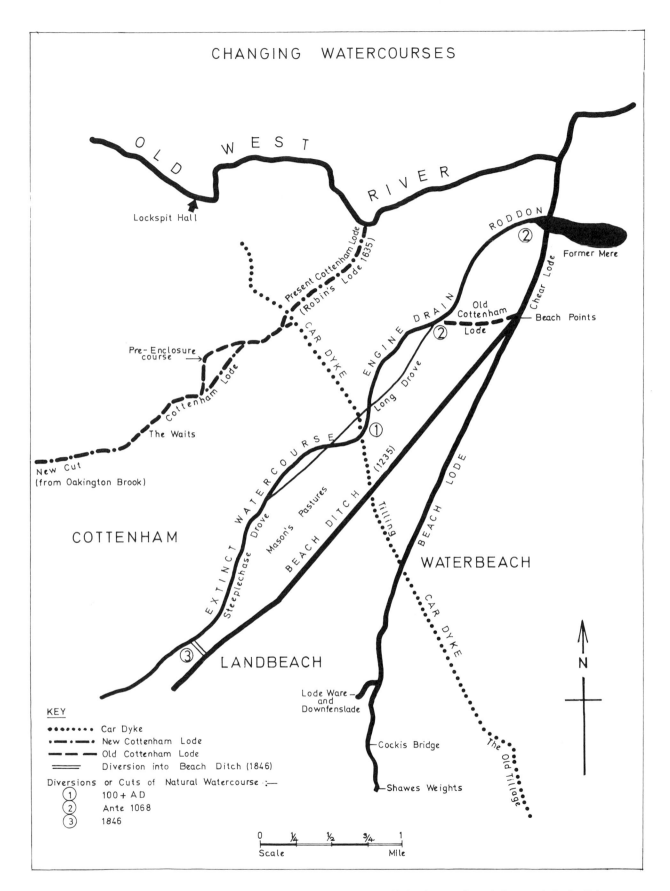

Fig. 20 Changing Watercourses. In the fenland most watercourses have been modified and man-made canals, for example the Car Dyke, may have gone wild and broken loose. The distinction between natural and artificial is therefore a matter of writing a history rather than making an identification, in the same way that an old house or church has a history rather than a date. *Reproduced by kind permission of Cambridge University Press from* Liable to Floods.

It was to this river that the barges of Landbeach, the waters of Beach Lode, Beach Tilling, and an unnamed vanished watercourse made their way. The waters of the last stream, which the Romans had used to fill the Car Dyke, were diverted in 1235 to form the Beach Ditch to define the fenny boundary between Landbeach and Cottenham. A hedge was planted at the same time, and gave its name in legal Latin of the time, *Haia*, to the new boundary path, Hay Lane.

The name 'Waits' which we meet also at St Ives, and which in Ramsey, by the Great Vowel Shift, has changed to 'Whytes', seems to be applied to any place where barges tied up for loading and unloading. The Whytes at Ramsey formed an immense mediaeval dock terminal, in a network of inland waterways that linked up with the smaller works of lesser market towns and villages. Matthew Parker left a description of the canals and the three docks of Landbeach in his field book of 1549.

50 Cuckoo Drift, about one mile west of Landbeach, marking the Cottenham-Oakington boundary and the old way to the Isle of Ely.

Item: the ditch lying on the north quarter of Frith Fen is called Landbeach Tilling, the said ditch lying betwen the Frith Fen and the High Fen, otherwise called the Common Fen.

Item: the ditch lying upon the east quarter of Frith Fen reckoning from the Barrs, otherwise called Prynceall, towards Landbeach, til ye come at Lode Ware over Down Fen Slade is called the Lode, and so forth to Madecroft, the ditch is called the Lode or the Common Drain, and from thence it goeth to a place called Cockis Bridge, and from thence to Shawes Weights. The said Cockis Bridge is nigh unto the common plot that is at this present in the town's hand. Shawes Weights is as well lying on the backside of Thomas Ward's house betwixt the said house and his little Grove.

Today, looking at long neglected or abandoned ditches like those which Parker described, of a minimum size that would take only the smallest narrow boats, suitable for village trade, it is hard for us to accept that these were part of an effective commercial network with international connections through the mediaeval fairs. The wide streets at Ramsey, and around the three-way bridge at Crowland, where today only the tarmac flows, were nodes in this system. It was 'navigation', the use of

Fig. 21 Matthew Parker's description of the ditches and docks in the village in 1549.

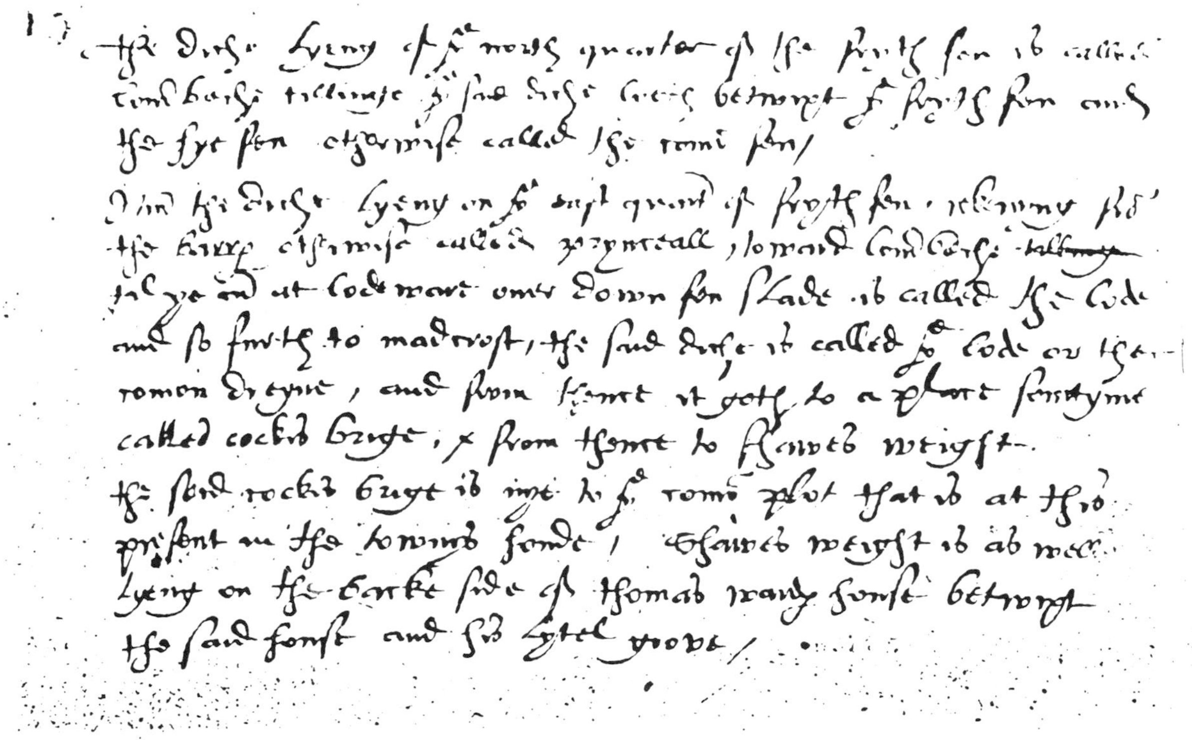

51 Ramsey, the Great
Whyte—mediaeval dockland.
The tiny canal ditches in
Landbeach offered easy
connection to great commercial
centres such as this.

these waterways, which determined Landbeach's position in the struggle
with the drainers. Where further north men and women turned out
armed with pitchforks and scythes, threatening to let the guts of anyone
who drove (i.e. animals over) their fen, Landbeach, with only a few acres
regularly inundated, enjoyed its mow fens and feeding grounds. In the
seventeenth century, through all the long years when drainers were at
work, the calendars of state papers are full of case after case of riot, or
breaking of drainage works by the fenland commoners afraid that their
commons would be taken from them, as in time they were.

Sometimes Landbeach seems to have been omitted from the surveys:
sometimes it seems to have serious flooding problems, and names like
Flood Lane, Flood Acre and Le Slo (the Slough) appear in the heart of
the village in the Middle Ages.

In the late eighteenth century, enthusiasm for enclosure and contempt
of open fields was spread by the propagandists of the Board of Agriculture, in their reports to the Board and their *General Views*, county by

county. They condemned common fields wherever they met them. Vancouver wrote his opinion on Landbeach in 1794:

> The soil south-east of the village is a gravelly loam proper for the culture of wheat, barley, oats, rye, peas, clover and turnips. North-east and towards the fens, is a strong well-stapled clay, lying upon a gault, and proper for the culture of wheat, beans, black oats and clover; of these there are about 800 acres, which are rented at 12s. per acre. The enclosures in severalty contain about 150 acres and are rented at twenty shillings per acre. The commons contain about one thousand acres, all of which, except about sixty acres, are

52 Crowland. Barges from Landbeach could once have floated under the bridge where there is now no water. Fen drainage eventually killed fen navigation.

high and dry. The soil of the lower parts is composed of strong earth and vegetable matter; of the higher parts, a loamy clay, lying upon a gault. The largest farm is held under a lease for fifteen years at one hundred and sixty pounds per annum. The common husbandry of two crops and a fallow is here the usual practice. An enclosure is greatly desired, under the encouragement of which very considerable improvements in the stock and husbandry of the parish would immediately take place; in which there are forty houses, fifty families and two hundred and fifty souls. The produce per acre is:

> 26 bushels of wheat
> 28 ditto barley
> 18 ditto peas and beans.

So the old order in the agriculture of Landbeach, and the social order that went with it, stood accused and condemned, and awaited only the execution.

Robert Masters had been converted to enclosure years before, and he left correspondence with Christopher Pemberton, the commissioner with the highest number of Parliamentary Enclosures to his credit, a record-breaking professional.

The book on Landbeach which Masters had projected to write to match his *Short Account of the Parish of Waterbeach*, was never written, but the comments on agriculture which he left for the intended volume are, if anything, more knowledgeable and sensitive than Vancouver's survey:

> Landbeach is of a good natural soil: yet although cultivated by judicious farmers, its produce is unequal to that of some neighbouring parishes. The quantity of arable land is less than 1,000 acres, whilst that of the enclosed pastures does not greatly exceed 100. There is a fine common nearly equal in quantity to the arable fields, which enclosed and well cultivated would be superior to them in quality, and not less profitable than in its present state, for feeding horses, cows, sheep, etc. The cows may well amount to upwards of 300, and the sheep to 2,600, dropping 900 lambs each year. These lambs are now obliged to be driven to a good distance for shelter and subsistence in the winter, at a very considerable trouble and expense; and the cows to be succoured by hay and fodder brought from the villages around. An enclosure of a very considerable part at the least of these commons would be highly beneficial, and will, I should hope, be soon adopted by those who are wise enough to discover their own true interest therein.

Masters never saw this promised land. The expense of buying out the common-rights of a group of Milton interests was too great, and it took time to get together sufficient indications of consent to enclose.

The Act was only passed in 1807, and on 26th September in that year the Commissioners began their work with a meeting at the 'Eagle and Child' in Cambridge, the favourite venue for Parliamentary Commissioners in this county. On the 15th December, 1813, they signed the Award.

It is hard to imagine the change in the local landscape, especially now that so many ancient elms have been lost. A few of the old canal banks and roadways still have venerable trees. The Mereway (Roman Road) in its southern portion has probably changed little since mediaeval times, except that the folk then might have removed and used much of the scrubby undergrowth and some of the lesser trees. But at the most open period of the Middle Ages there would have been more driftways carrying shrubs and some trees right out into the heart of all the fields. But for some time after the Award, before hedges grew, and after what trees there were had been largely felled for fencing, the fields would have looked much like a prairie.

Slowly, especially by steam ploughing between the two World Wars, the patched corduroy pattern of ridge and furrow in the furlongs was smoothed out. Straight fences, ditches, paths and roads replaced the organic pattern of the old field ways: access to the countryside began to be lost to all but the farmers. Aerial photography can still detect much of this past, but the steam ploughing still looks like an attempt by a giant to erase all the previous signs of life by scribbling on an enormous scale. Similarly, time and the generations which seized their main chances have done much, through statute and precedent, to change the pattern of land-holding. But when we stand back and look hard, we can still detect something of the frame that Domesday pressed on the community nine hundred years ago.

The complicated pattern of the ploughman's ridge and furrow began to disappear in time: the lawyers' tangle of strips in divers hands was disentangled. But, *plus ça change*, in its new shapes the land was still distinguished by manor and perhaps status. The lord of Milton, its rector and vicar, the Provost, Fellows and Scholars of King's College, Cambridge, were all awarded allotments to compensate for their old common rights which they had used effectively against earlier attempts at enclosure.

The overseers of the poor and the surveyors of the highways received what was the equivalent of their small endowments in land. Some of the villagers held land under the manor of Waterbeach cum Denney, and

53 Landbeach and environs, looking south. In the soil marks in the field in the foreground, the north end of Frith Fen, parallel dark lines of silted ditches reveal Roman roads and droveways. Little is known of the enclosures that show up in the area. The tree-lined ditches coming in from the left are the two branches of the mediaeval canals. *Cambridge University Collection: copyright reserved.*

this, like other property from the earliest days, went into the pool for an equivalent enclosed allocation.

The rector had big interests for tithe, common-rights and sheepwalk as well as glebe, but by far the largest part was identified as being held under the manor of Chamberlains or Brays. Some of the latter had changed its title to the Trustees of the Worts Charity Estate, that the lord of the manor of Brays had made from that manor nearly a century before. Most of the manorial land was identified as freehold or copyhold, and so it went on until changes in the statutes in the period between the Wars made copyhold obsolete. John Hemington, who held one of the larger farms, received eleven allotments copyhold of Chamberlains and one copyhold of Waterbeach cum Denney. It was good land, and no worse for its origins, or for its centuries under Domesday labels.

*   *   *

Parliamentary Enclosure came late to most of Cambridgeshire. It reached Landbeach only in the nineteenth century. Burroughes was the rector who had to deal with it, and he also was something of a man on the spot for the College and its interests as lord of the manor. Burroughes was very much an enthusiast for enclosure.

When he came to the living in Landbeach he set out to find his glebe in the open fields with the aid of one of the old field books. In spite of the accuracy of his source, some of the land seemed to be lost. Burroughes was determined to safeguard it for the future. As each field came into its fallow season, Burroughes took the opportunity to mark each rectory strip with new oak 'dowells'. Each of these had an anchor piece, and they were painted and given appropriate lettering. In the 1799 accounts appears:

> 35 oak land-marks anchored at the bottom, put down in Millfield (consisting of 18 acres of glebe land but lying in 35 different pieces).
> Cost of posts 1s.0d. each   £1:15:00
> Putting oak anchors to each, digging holes, workmanship,
> lettering and painting 1s.0d.   £1:15:00

In 1800 he paid for 21 oak posts for glebe in Scachbow field, and 24 for Banworth. In the same set of accounts he recorded the purchase of bricks and tiles to construct the bay window in the house. While concerned to claim the full share of glebe in the new allotment, he appears to have had great expectations as to the profitability of enclosure. For the year ended Lady Day, 1808, he considered his overall position as rector: 'This sum, £54-8-5d., I have made in one year of the rectory by strict attention to the business of a farmer, but the new allotted lands in lieu of tithe etc. may be let for more than this sum and all trouble saved to the rector.'

The allotment of land in lieu of tithe was particularly helpful to the parson: he avoided the embarrassment of having to collect goods in kind, or the unpopularity of an annual rent-charge in lieu of tithe. Just what the conversion of country priests into rentiers did for the Church of England it is hard to say. He ceased to be a farmer among farmers, and his great interest in the land was to see that his tenants farmed the land properly, observing the terms of the lease, keeping to the proper rotations, ensuring that the land stayed clean and in good heart and that expensive fences and buildings were maintained. The prudent landlord-rector would give an eye to all this. He might also provide an extra pair of eyes for the lord of the manor in which he had his own part.

Projects for draining the fens were part of the fever of speculative investment in schemes to get rich quickly. As early as 1597 a twenty-one year monopoly of draining was granted. On the one hand such monopolies need to be considered with patents for absurd schemes for perpetual motion, which characterise the period, and on the other, with such ventures as the Plymouth and Virginia Companies for colonising the New World. Sir Miles Sandys was out to get land either in the New World or from drainage schemes in the North Cambridgeshire fens. Such was the type of landlord and speculator who pressed for the draining. In the early days the Cromwell family were very much involved. In 1618 extensive powers to improve drainage and navigation were given to: Sir Oliver Cromwell, bt., Sir John Cutts, bt., Sir Simeon Steward, kt., Sir Philip Cromwell, kt., Henry Cromwell Sr., Henry Kervile, Thos Audley, John Fynnes, A.M., Francis Brone, Robert Audley, Humphrey Gordon, Esq., Robert Buteler. Such a small commission seems well provided with Cromwells.

By 1631 the King had found that the multitude of the Commissioners preferred their little benefit before the general good. He had begun to have such suspicions years before, and made the affair a matter of state, hoping to make money himself from the project. But lack of capital prevented him from effective participation. The eventual solution was the Bedford Level Corporation and Cornelius Vermuyden, the Dutch drainage engineer.

Vermuyden was only one of a number of competing drainage engineers from Holland who hoped to make fortunes from draining the fens. After several years of quarrelling and back-biting among interested parties, which only seemed to hinder, if not prevent, all progress, Vermuyden found employment for his talents between 1626 and 1630 in draining Hatfield Chase. Then he quickly rose to the top rank of engineering reputation by mounting a direct attack on the plans of his most formidable Dutch rival, Westerdyke. The latter was defeated but not destroyed, and came back to harry Vermuyden again when he, in his turn, was under criticism.

By the so-called 'Lynn Law' of 1637, the work was declared completed, but disastrous flooding soon showed that this was manifestly not so, and the Civil War held up any further attempt for some years. Under the

Commonwealth, work was resumed on the authority of the so-called 'pretended Act' of 1649, which could only acquire strict legal force when authorised by Royal Assent. This placed the responsibility for draining the fens on the shoulders of the Bedford Level Corporation. The Russell family, which produced the Earls and Dukes of Bedford, were the largest landowners in the area, and so public works were to be achieved by giving private interest the chance and duty of pursuing its own interests. Vermuyden had another struggle with Westerdyke to retain control over the renewed works, and further battles, not entirely successful, to obtain the remuneration to which he felt entitled.

In the very long run, i.e. by the present day, the fenmen may have been right. Their complaint of 1622: 'Their schemes are impracticable: fens were made fens and must ever continue such, and are useful in multiplying fowl and fish, and producing turf etc,' sounds very much like the International Conference on Wetlands which, a few years ago, declared that wherever wetlands had been drained the biological potential (capacity to support life) had fallen.

The difficulty of draining the fens arose from the fact that the water gathered up by an enormous catchment area was made to pass through a

54 Mediaeval canal at the north end of the village.

159

low area with scarcely any gradient, to the sea, and that as a consequence, meeting the tides head on, the outfalls silted up. The experts of the time, not least Verymuyden himself, tackled the problem by straightening and deepening the rivers to speed up the flow and so increase the effectiveness with which they scoured their own beds. Vermuyden had other parts to his scheme, but was not allowed to carry them out, and at the first real test the rivers burst and the country flooded again. The catchwater drain, which Vermuyden wanted to put around the whole fen area, was never implemented even in principle until after the flood of 1947. In the midst of such acrimony Vermuyden supplemented the old works with new. The essence of the novelty was that the rivers were supported by washes, created by building the embankments well back from the river, and even digging a parallel river as an alternative with a sluice to divert floodwaters to the appropriate channel into what amounted to an enormous reservoir, which could hold much more than the old river systems ever could, until the conditions of tide and wind made it safe to let the water out to the sea.

To the extent that this was successful, a new problem was created. The peat that was exposed dried and shrank, oxidised and blew away. The level of the surface dropped, became water-logged and reverted to fen. Windmills (imitating the Dutch once again) were installed to lift water from the fens to the drains. This succeeded until even gangs of windmills, each lifting water to its neighbour, reached the point where two systems of drainage were working together but growing further apart—a low-level system in the fields, and a high-level system to the sea in banks above them. By the late eighteenth century even the gang lifting was patently failing, especially since, as dependence on windmills increased, so did the erratic nature of the wind extract a heavier and heavier toll. Then came the Industrial Revolution, and the steam-pumps which had been invented to drain the Cornish mines were installed in the fen. The two which did most to keep Landbeach safe were Smithy Fen Engine, which began in 1846, and the Stretham Beam Engine (1831) which may still be inspected today.

Steam turned the fen from chancy oats-growing country to excellent wheat land. The riches that seventeenth-century visitors had seen in patches of drained fen seemed to have been realised over the whole area drained by steam power. First diesel, which could be started more easily and more quickly in emergency than steam, and then, much better still, electric pumping with instant start and automatic control, took over, and worked within the arc of the catchwater drain. All seemed at last safe. Only the peat seems to be vanishing faster than ever, and an intractable, infertile blue clay emerging to the surface.

14

The Road to the Isle

Fragments of the Roman road were used by travellers on foot and on horseback from Cambridge to the Isle of Ely, but mostly they went on a path, by permission only, just inside the parish boundary between Landbeach and Waterbeach, going from Milton to Goose Hall and on by Stretham Ferry.

The period that saw Masters' changes to the Rectory, from a farmhouse with a clergy wing to a country gentleman's residence, would have found a carriage, rather than barge or horseback, a more proper means of transport and travel for senior clergy of the diocese or of Cambridge University.

In 1757, Bentham, the historian of Ely Cathedral, floated the idea that there was an old road from Cambridge to Ely which might be made up into a carriage road. The road at that time was a thing of shreds and patches, or as the Act was to declare, 'in some parts narrow and incommodious, and others annoyed by water for want of bridges'. The Act of 1763 was passed to remedy this situation, but it neither ordered a new road nor authorised the making up and improvement of the old Roman road. Instead it provided for the repairing, widening and turning of the road that had grown up, partly by permission, and partly by usage—the right-hand branch, as it was designated, as if everyone stood permanently in Cambridge, looking towards Ely. Perhaps this was not so odd if we examine a list of commissioners, dated probably about 1795. It contains sixteen heads of Cambridge Colleges, including the Vice-Chancellor, the Mayor of Cambridge and twelve Aldermen, eight Prebendaries of Ely, and twenty-one Commissioners Resident at Ely.

Led by their rector, once more, the villagers of Landbeach objected. The new road, which in any case was useless in winter in its first years

55 The village smithy as it appeared on its old site at the cross-roads. It was removed before the First World War to the Plague House, where the wheelwright's shop and tools, sawpit and forge, can all be remembered before the recent restoration.

owing to flooding, went through valuable meadow as well as commons, near the parish boundary, distant from the homes of the Landbeach commoners, but vulnerable and attractive to undesirable characters, pickers up of unconsidered trifles. The pits which had been left by those who dug gravel for the road were unguarded traps for the villagers' animals. It was not only useless for Landbeach where the other road would have been a great convenience, but it introduced four miles of road into the parish where there had been but two. Adding injury to insult, it had to be maintained by parish labour from Landbeach.

The promoters of the turnpike managed, without Masters getting wind of it, to introduce another bill and get it passed, doubling the parish labour due from the good inhabitants of Landbeach. It must have taken a remarkable security operation to keep such news from Masters' ears.

The Enclosure Commissioners for Landbeach, when making their Award, suggested that Akeman Street should be made up from the corner of Cockfen Lane to the highway between Milton and Impington, but nothing was done at the time. The opening of the railway at Histon raised the question again, since such a road would shorten the journey from Worts Farm and Rectory Farm to the new railhead. Worts Trustees called a public meeting to discuss whether there would be sufficient support to carry out such a scheme by public subscription, and offered £300. The rector paid £60. No one else seemed to be interested, nor could it help anyone else.

Partial making up from Cockfens south, for about half the roadway, was carried out at a cost of £500. Worts increased their subscription to cover most of the balance. This improved part is now concreted, but further south to the main road, overgrown with bushes and trees, the Greenway, still usually termed Mereway, is the most romantic walk left in the village, impassable in wet seasons, and the most hazardous way we have for agricultural machinery which gets heavier year by year. It is the only survival of the numerous driftways, which led out to the heart of all the open fields before the others were swept away by enclosure.

A journalist of the Cambridge Independent Press in 1897 produced an article on Landbeach, which incidentally gives an interesting picture of the turnpike at that time: 'Along the road at intervals, more or less irregular, are to be met the carts of carriers, the pedlars and on market day especially it is most lively with market gardeners on the way to Cambridge.'

The journalist was surprised to meet a street singer with a fine tenor voice, accompanying himself on an accordion. We should be, too. Today it would be more likely to be a powerful machine 'doing a ton on the A10'.

*   *   *

There are no old houses in the village out near the turnpike road. The furthest out that that side developed before the Civil War appears to be Unwins, about a hundred yards east of the cross-roads. There is just one other possibility; part of the structure of the older part of the 'Slap-Up' Inn may well be earlier than is generally suspected. Changes in the buildings make dating hazardous; what we are confronted with is fragments of a history rather than a date. One of the points of interest very common among our old houses is that so many of them which have their original axial chimney stack, in true seventeenth-century style, have also one or two small square gable end chimneys. Sometimes these have been removed again later. In shape, brick and plan they are typical of the eighteenth century, and there is a type of small eighteenth-century cottage which had such a small stack also placed axially between two different-sized rooms, only one of which need be heated. This type was

163

sometimes divided also, and a second fireplace might again be added at the gable end.

These additional chimneys are outward and visible signs of a massive social change. Once again population was increasing at great speed. One of the ways of housing new families was to increase the number of units of accommodation by sub-dividing existing housing, or putting more than one family into as many houses as could be made available for lower standard homes.

The entry for our two manors in the Domesday Book suggested a population of about 160–175, and the Hundred Rolls suggested that in the two centuries after Domesday the population in Landbeach, and many other Cambridgeshire villages, had all but doubled. But after the Black Death the population does not seem to have passed the figure of the Hundred Rolls of 1278–9 until early in the nineteenth century. The first census figure of 1801 was still below, but other sources suggest it was rising fast, soon to rise above the probable 290 of the Hundred Rolls, which must have been nearly a peak.

The census figures show something of the pressure of population on accommodation. In 1811 the village had 48 houses and 61 families: in 1821 it had 47 houses and 80 families. Only 25 families had a house to themselves, and at the other extreme two houses tried to house four families each. This sort of picture is probably not far wrong, as the fate of the older houses suggests. The addition and removal of flues means that practically all houses for labourers were being reduced to 'one up and one down', to squeeze the maximum of families into existing accommodation.

The great change in the village, associated with the decrease in opportunities for employment and the displacement of workers by machinery on the farm, had not yet begun in Landbeach by the census of 1811. Of the 61 families recorded in that year, 46 were reported as being mainly engaged in agriculture, and only nine in trade. These are simple figures, but they indicate the villager's dependence on the farmers, and his lack of any sort of bargaining power. The farmer was tempted to exploit this, because he was conscious of the ever-rising Poor Rates which he had to pay.

During the Revolutionary and Napoleonic Wars there was much money to be made from the production of food. 'Speed the Plough' was urged, as in later wars, 'Dig for Victory'. This seems to have met with response in Landbeach. Shallow ridge and furrow in such places as the present recreation ground and some of the manorial closes seems to belong to this period and does not figure in the older field books. There are other possible indications in the dry parts of Frith Fen of this 'War Agriculture'.

Fig. 22 From Robert Masters' *Collectanea de Landbeach*, an attempt in 1781 at aggregative analysis.

Landbeach

From 1688			From 1730			From 1750		
Bapt.	Mar.	Bur.	Bapt.	Mar.	Bur.	Bapt.	Mar.	Bur.
6	2	3	8	1	16	8	2	5
7	3	6	10	—	8	9	2	10
9	1	9	7	1	6	8	—	6
14	3	11	10	3	5	6	1	5
9	1	8	7	1	4	5	1	5
8	2	5	10	1	5	8	4	9
5	1	6	5	3	10	4	2	8
9	2	6	5	1	12	7	—	11
13	3	11	11	—	6	7	1	—
11	4	4	6	4	9	5	4	4
10	2	8	4	2	5	6	4	5
11	1	9	4	—	6	9	—	7
11	1	8	8	2	10	8	1	2
11	2	6	3	1	3	11	1	9
8	2	3	7	1	6	8	1	7
12	1	4	5	1	6	5	3	5
14	3	8	6	1	6	8	—	2
7	1	5	4	1	5	11	—	7
10	1	9	7	1	5	8	5	5
12	2	6	5	—	5	11	1	5
Tot. 20 yrs. 197	38	135	132	25	137	152	34	117

5 3 7 1781.
5 0 8 1780

Families in 1781 — 49 —
Inhabitants — 215 —
Houses charged to Windows 25 — not charged 24 in all 49.

165

But the labourers of Landbeach, who do not seem to have shared in the wartime prosperity of their masters, likewise do not seem to have suffered from wild excesses of patriotism.

In the rector's *Account of the Parish of Landbeach*, 1795, called for by the Militia Act, total population is given as 239, of whom 67 were males between 15 and 60 years of age. The number serving in a military capacity was only 3. This is in stark contrast to the lists of those who served and died from the village in the two World Wars.

The story of village after village in the nineteenth century is the story of the drift from the land, and this continued and was resumed sharply after the First World War. The last phase has come with the internal combustion engine. This has carried further the replacement of man-power on the land but soon after allowed the re-occupation of villages as dormitories. Old ways in country life, some with unbelievably deep roots, began to vanish early in these changes.

John Denson of Waterbeach, in his *A Peasant's Voice to Landowners* (Cambridge, 1830), wrote the elegy of the customary pattern of rural life that he saw fade, the common life with common fields and common pasture, and many common pleasures, like the annual festivals such as May Day.

Denson also tells of the social gulf which he saw grow so rapidly in his generation between the farmers' families and the labourers'. Pianos in the farmhouse parlour were not only the symbol but almost the instruments of the separation of the two classes. The young people from the farmhouse no longer danced with the young people from the cottages: they no longer went to the same dances.

When strong feeling and resentment was running below the surface, the farmer was very vulnerable in his timber-framed farmhouse and farmbuildings, mostly with thatched roofs. There is an account in one of the registers:

A dreadful fire happened on Good Friday 1798 about 6 o'clock in the morning, which consumed all the barns, stables and outhouses, implements of husbandry, grain, straw, belonging to *John Foote*, to a very considerable amount. The wind was very high and was blowing nearly south, and had it not providentially turned a few points to the west during the violence of the fire, the whole village would probably have been destroyed.

One barn in an adjoining farm yard, belonging to Mary Taylor, was burnt down by the communication of the flames.

At this date such a happening could be recorded by the parson without a hint that anything but Act of God was involved. Fifty years on, the

56 A former Post Office with a semi-basement, this house has all the appearance of a typical town house.

57 The Black Bull has ceased to be a pub but has acquired a mascot.

assumption would be made almost automatically that a fire-raiser was loose in the village. Gardener's *Directory* of 1851 noted of Landbeach, 'No less than three attempts at incendiarism have been lately made in or near the village.' It was much worse in Cottenham.

Until the onset of the great depression in agriculture, in the early 1870s, the number of pubs seems to have been increasing. Gardener's *Directory* for 1851 lists six licensed victuallers: the Bricklayer's Arms, the Black Bull, the Bower, the Windmill, the Coach and Horses and the Queen Adelaide, and one beer retailer. In 1864 Kelly's *Directory* added the 'Slap-Up' Inn and the British Queen. Today one only remains, the 'Slap-Up', and that is much nearer to the main village at Waterbeach than to the main part of Landbeach. The village does its best with a club.

Well before the agricultural depression, emigration had begun to take a hold in the Cambridgeshire countryside. The turn-over of surnames was rapid. This exaggerates the change in families, because inheritance down the female line looks the same as a family moving out. A surname may disappear with marriage, but if the groom comes to live in his wife's village, the family in effect stays. But even allowing for this, the nineteenth century saw a great loss of the old families. Now one generation of residence makes an old village family and two generations an ancient one. A comparison between the listings of 1781 and 1851 shows that 22 of the surnames of 1781 have disappeared by 1851; 26 survived; and there were 44 new names by 1851.

15

The Survivors

The year of the ninth centenary of the Domesday Survey is a good time to ponder once again on what the Survey did to England, and how much of this is with us today. What did the Normans achieve in England?

They completed and riveted on to the English countryside the system of land-ownership, organised in manors held ultimately of the Monarch. Whether the result of policy, or merely the pressures of daily watching and trying to satisfy his greedy followers, William's grants of land left most of the new Norman overlords with scattered collections of property; and, by accident rather than intent, in parts of the country like the fen edge with easy water transport, such estates could be developed into large-scale agricultural enterprises, and such need did arise from the extra mouths that needed feeding in the thirteenth century. The canal network in eastern England at that time was invaluable to the high farming landlords.

This system of water transport appears originally to have begun for the building of churches, parochial and monastic, and then to have developed for commerce. In the Middle Ages, there was in the tiny village of Landbeach a deepwater dock, Down Fen Slade, where the building stone could be unloaded close to the church and principal manor house. The other two docks, Cockis Bridge and Shawes Weights, were close at hand at the back of peasant tofts. Some networks of canals, and some building of stone churches, had begun before the Normans came, but once again they completed what they found.

William liked to use the strength of the Church to supplement the State and, where convenient, moved the centres of administration of Church and State close together; and parallel, perhaps not by design but for convenience, lordship of the manor and patronage of the parish church

58 An old, unglazed window
in the former Black Bull. Before
the brick skin was added, this
was an outside window.

59 Landbeach in the twentieth
century, an amalgam of many
generations and styles. On the
left the timber-framed tradition
as it developed in the
eighteenth century; on the
right the attractive,
unpretentious architecture of
the early nineteenth century,
which used a particularly
pleasant local brick.

tended to go together. By the time Corpus Christi College became the lords of the Chamberlains manor, only the alternative presentation went to them, but they soon acquired the other turn as well. More than six hundred years later, Chamberlains manor has lost the alternative presentation to enable the living to be held in plurality with Waterbeach.

Ever since Domesday until very recently, manors were the key to landownership. Most of them survived the property lottery of the sixteenth century and, in spite of the new powers in local government, we saw the manor court in Landbeach still directing the day-to-day operation of the open fields and commons and the conservation of the village, as late as the reign of Edward VI. Eventually Parliamentary Enclosure wiped the pattern of our common fields from the landscape, a pattern that went back far beyond what the memory of any man could recall. But the new pattern was a rearrangement into something simpler, into blocks of land according to whether they were Chamberlains or Brays, and in each case free or copyhold. The nineteenth century local government reforms prepared the way for abolition of copyhold and of manors. But it was not a simple move towards democracy: we have only to think of Robert Masters as Pooh Bah at the commoners' meeting, which surely should be the most democratic village gathering of the time. A close look at Masters' portrait in the church almost seems to bring the comment, 'Manor and parish; Church and State. *C'est moi!*'

Even the setting up of parish councils did not immediately solve the problem of how to run village affairs. The reporter who visited Landbeach in 1897 found that the parish council had been run by a single family oligarchy since its inception, and had managed to prevent any expenditure of parish rates apart from the initial election expenses of £5.

To plot the old open field patterns of the village one needs an aeroplane, or at least a good set of air photographs, but a glance at the Enclosure Award Map, which is small enough to have the schedule of every scrap of land in its top right-hand quarter, reveals both manors in full. Since the buying up of the Worts property by the County Council, the lords of both manors are Immortal Corporations, and so, in spite of the abolition of manors, ours refuse to die.

Index

Numbers in italics refer to illustrations